Praise f

I have read tons of self-help books and articles and been through positive thinking classes and they have all had temporary effects then, ultimately, fallen short. Jim Straw's books and courses, loaded with common sense and practical advice and clear-cut directions, are the only ones I've found which have consistently earned me good profits. Jim is the "Real Deal."

—*Marilyn Combs*
Partners in Business
Phoenix, Arizona

Do you seek the real secret of success? You will find that and more in this book. J.F. Straw lives what he teaches. Whether for your business or for any other endeavor in life, you can learn something from him. You may never have heard of Jim Straw before, yet the simple method he reveals here has made him one of the most all-around successful men who has ever lived. This book probably should be required reading no later than eighth grade in every school district in America. In short: read the book, apply it, and better your life.

—*M.B. Leibowitz, PhD*

Over the years I've added at least one-hundred dollars each business day in take home for every new idea I gain from your practical insights.

—*Justin Hitt*
Publisher, Inside Strategic Relations
Business Development Consultant

J.F. (Jim) Straw is a living legend among informed marketers of every kind. Perhaps because he has sold just about everything in his 40+ years of being in business. Which all by itself is a testimony of super success. He is now still doing what he preaches and loves best: writing , publishing, and teaching others (the noblest profession of them all). His secrets, methods, and recipes for success have made his exceptionally rich life the one to be emulated and hopefully imitated.

—*Mike DiBiano*
www.tollgatepositions.com

---

* In most books that are published, the people who praise the book or author are usually reviewers, people who are "reciprocating" for the author (or publisher), or people who want to be associated with a book. The testimonials included here are a little different: they were written not by "names" or reviewers; rather, they are the people who perhaps know Mr. Straw best: his clients, customers, and students.

I have known Jim Straw for over 30 years now. What separates Jim Straw from many business leaders in his field is that he is dedicated to what he does best: helping people.

—*William Lucas*
Ontario, Canada

Jim has hit the nail on the head. You can do all the psychic (or magick) work you like, but if it's all in your head, it ain't taking you nowhere. The art, as Jim so astutely points out, is to back up your psychic/magick work with real world efforts. It is this that brings you the edge—and will bring success. Guaranteed!

—*Jimmy Lee Shreeve*
http://doktorsnake.com

I was so fed up with all of the famous, swollen-headed, inaccessible business coaches. Then, thankfully, I learned of Jim Straw. I hate to say this, but Jim Straw is probably the last of his breed: a kindly, wise mentor who keeps his promises and keeps on teaching. Thank you, Jim.

—*Jeff Trewhella*

Jim Straw has lived, done, and experienced what he writes about. If you want "fluff," "bluff," and "bullstuff," then there are plenty of "authors" out there more than willing to sell you their "bullstuff" and laugh all the way to the bank. Jim Straw will tell you how he's actually done it. Isn't that what you really want and need?

—*Father M.*

You are the "real deal" in a world full of entrepreneurial charlatans.

—*Jack Jakoubek*

I like the way you write and explain things. Thanks, Jim, for the truth I sense in you.

—*Thom*

Bottom line: I trust Jim and I am looking forward to working with him.

—*Merial Jones*

Mustard Seeds, Shovels, & Mountains

How to Succeed Using Your Physio-Psychic Power

KALLISTI PUBLISHING
Wilkes-Barre, PA

"The Books You Need to Read to Succeed"
Kallisti Publishing
332 Center Street
Wilkes-Barre, PA 18702
Phone (570) 825-3598 • Fax (419) 781-1907
www.kallistipublishing.com

Kallisti Publishing's titles may be bulk purchased for business
or promotional use or for special sales. Please contact Kallisti
Publishing for more information.

Kallisti Publishing and its logo are trademarks of Kallisti Publishing.

10 9 8 7 6 5 4 3 2 1

ISBN **0-9848162-0-8**
ISBN-13 **978-0-9848162-0-0**
Library of Congress Control Number: **2012930722**

DESIGNED & PRINTED IN THE UNITED STATES OF AMERICA

In Loving Memory
Delores Satterfield Straw
My beloved wife for over 42 years.
Since her death on June 9, 2009,
I have grown somewhat
accustomed to being alone.
The lonliness, however, persists…

**My Personal Philosophy
in Business and Life**
*Hand-written on a slip of yellowing paper
that has been in the top drawer of my desk
for nearly 40 years.
Where it came from, I do not know.
Who said it originally, I do not know.
When I transcribed it and put it in my desk, I do not know.
It simply says…*
"Let him who would be great among you be servant to all."

$\mathcal{T}$able of $\mathcal{C}$ontents

Put it before them briefly so they will read it, clearly so they will appreciate it, picturesquely so they will remember it and, above all, accurately so they will be guided by its light.

—Joseph Pulitzer

$\mathcal{F}$oreword

When you learned that 2 + 2 = 4, you gained a useful piece of *information*. When you learned that 2 apples + 2 apples = 4 apples, but 2 apples + 2 oranges = 2 apples and 2 oranges, or 2 pairs of fruit, or 4 fruits; you have gained all-important *knowledge*.

Information is nice to know. It lets you answer the questions on tests or when watching TV game shows. But, until you learn to use that information in a practical application, it isn't knowledge.

Any child of two or three years of age can tell you that 2 + 2 = 4. They have heard it repeated over and over until they can repeat it themselves. But, when confronted with four apples, they are at a loss to apply that information.

The same holds true for older students (and even adults) who can readily tell you that Einstein's Theory of Relativity can be expressed by the formula $E=MC^2$. Until they know what the E, M, and C stand for and can use the formula in a practical application, it is only information, not knowledge.

A fine line exists between information and knowledge. That fine line is nothing more than *use*. You can memorize bits and pieces of information all day, every day, but until you actually use that information, it is not knowledge. Once used, information becomes knowledge and, thereby, power.

Successful people, whether they be self-employed or wage-earners, executive or common laborer, are seekers after knowledge. They absorb information from every direction. The information they can use becomes knowledge, while the information they have no apparent use for is simply stored on the chance that someday it may become useful.

Unsuccessful people, on the other hand, claim to be seekers of knowledge, but they believe that knowledge itself can be imparted. Because the books they read, the courses they take, and the plans they buy contain only *information*, they are forever disappointed. Because it is *only information* and not the "knowledge" they thought they were going to get, they never use the information and, thereby, the knowledge they sought is lost to them forever.

Since I am the author of a great many books, booklets, reports, articles, and editorials about success and making and using money (somewhere over 700 so far), those people stick out like sore-thumbs on my customer lists. They write me long letters detailing their trials and tribulations and explain to me just why the information won't work for them. Not one ever writes "I used the information and it didn't work." Had they ever used the information, that information would have turned into knowledge and they could have reaped the rewards they have coveted for so long.

If there was a way I could force those people to use the information they have, I could literally *guarantee* their success. And, in those few cases over the years where I have been able to shame or intimidate people into actually using the information I have provided, those people have achieved successes they had only dreamed were possible.

The *Rules of Success* used by successful people and businesses since the beginning of time have never really changed. Those rules have been written down for all to read, learn, and use, but they appear as information only and can only be changed to knowledge by use. If there were a way to force every person and every business to use those known and proven rules of success, there would be *no* unsuccessful people or businesses in the world.

Statistically, 90% of small businesses fail and 90% of people live a life of sustained mediocrity—simply because they will not use the information available to them.

In your quest for financial independence you *must* learn to force yourself to *use* the information you have at your disposal. No one but *you* is going to force you to assume that responsibility.

Of course, some smart aleck reading this is going to say, "Yeah! But, I'm not going to use any bad information."

Granted, there is bad (counter-productive) information out

there. But, there is no way of telling good information from bad information *until you try it*. Judging the value of information without using it is like trying to judge the flavor of a pie without ever tasting it.

If you learn nothing else from this book, learn that **information only becomes knowledge when you use it and the information you have used or failed to use in the past is the reason you are where you are today.**

You can be your best friend—or your worst enemy. No one forces you to be what you are or do what you do (or don't do). What you have today is a direct result of what you did yesterday. What you will have tomorrow will be a direct result of what you do (or don't do) today.

It's up to you...

I bargained with life for a penny
And life would pay no more
However I begged at evening
When I counted my scanty store

For life is a just employer
He gives you what you ask
But once you have set the wages
Why, you must bear the task

I worked for a menial's hire
Only to learn dismayed
That any wage I had asked of life
Life would have willing paid.

—Jessie B. Rittenhouse

*I*ntroduction

*D*uring my lifetime, I have quaffed weak coffee from tin cans in hobo jungles beneath railroad trestles; chugged warm beer from canteen cups in the jungles of Southeast Asia; and sipped fine wine from exquisite crystal goblets in palatial homes around the world. All were instances befitting my station in life at the time.

I have had more money that I could carry and I have been completely and total without money; but I have never been poor. Poverty is a state of mind, not the state of your pocketbook.

Born in Oklahoma and reared on farms in Oklahoma, Missouri, and Kansas, I began my career in business at the age of nine when I sold my first cans of Cloverleaf Salve and copies of *GRIT* newspaper. My business career progressed through direct selling, service contracting, wholesale merchandising, entertainment (I was a professional trumpet player, vocalist, and radio announcer), freight forwarding, import/export, retail merchandising, warehousing, real estate, electronics manufacturing, finder's fees, close-out merchandising, financial brokerage, business consulting, steel fabrication, gold mining, coal mining, banking, mail order, writing, and publishing.

When I started doing business automobiles only had one headlight on each side, gasoline was 14¢ a gallon, milk was 25¢ a gallon, cigarettes were 11¢ a pack and $1 a carton, and grown men worked 40 hours a week for $44 (but you could buy a full shopping cart of groceries enough to last two weeks for about $25).

My first telephone number was 29W3.

In high school, there were 33 students in my class—16 boys and 17 girls. Being an absolute democracy, the girls won every issue we voted on unless Curt could get Linda to vote our way.

I went to college carrying a double-major: music and mathematics. Dropped out my sophomore year when the Dean of Men found out I was making more money than the President of the college and advised me to "just go do what you do and hire some of the students we graduate."

Went into the Army. I was the oldest man in my unit, even older than the Captain. Served in Vietnam. Lots of memories there, good and bad.

I remember the old business men who had shared their experiences with me and taught me how to do what they had done. I couldn't have done it without them.

Learned my most valuable lessons from my failures. My successes never really taught me much of anything. My successes were simply based upon what I had learned from my failures.

All in all, it was a wonderful fifty years. I'm looking forward to the next fifty.

Over the past 37 years, I have written well over 700 books, booklets, manuals, reports, courses and articles about doing business—all based on my own personal, hands-on experience. My writings are specific methods, techniques, and approaches to doing business that anyone can use to start or expand their business.

As a mail order marketer, I sold products and services to over 700,000 customers worldwide. Everything from beauty supplies to heavy equipment; burglar alarms to sleeping bags; fishing lures to women's wigs; automobiles to wheelchairs; investment opportunities to seafood; consulting services to "how-to" courses…. All by mail order.

Over the past fifty-plus years in the business arenas of the world, I have been asked countless times, "What are the secrets of your success?"

I hate to tell you this, but…

There are no "secrets" to success.

As a matter of fact, my Daddy used to say, "There really aren't any secrets in this old world. Only things you don't happen to know right now."

Over the past nearly fifty years, I have added, "Even after you learn what you didn't know, it still remains a secret until you actually do it successfully."

Therein lies the problem.

Most people who say they want to succeed go around all their life looking for some "secret" that people like me are sure to know. They just know that if they ever learned that "secret" they would be successful, too.

It ain't gonna happen, because there are no secrets.

All they need to do is start doing something. That's all it takes. Once they start really doing something—other than searching for the "secret" to success—whatever they are doing will expand and grow into the success for which they couldn't find the secret.

Over the past years in business, I have heard it thousands upon thousands of times from success secret seekers. "I ain't gonna get into no nickel and dime business. I want to make millions, not nickels and dimes."

So, they keep buying what they think are "secrets." They never do anything longer than it takes to find out they didn't learn any secrets, they just learned how to work at something. Then, they go on to the next "secret," hoping against hope that the new "secret" will give them the success they seek (without doing anything other than knowing the "secret").

The funny thing is, they all seem to think they are better than me and all the other successful people around the world because they honestly believe that I just woke up one morning, learned the secret, and made a fortune. When, in pure fact, I started selling nickel and dime items, door to door, in my youth, selling one item to one customer, one sale at a time, making a nickel or a dime on each sale.

As I matured, my endeavors expanded and grew, changed course, adapted to the ever changing economy, moved onward and upward. Each instance of my growth predicated upon providing what my potential customers needed or wanted. Making sure that I gave more value in return for the value I received and, even today, I still sell one item to one customer, one sale at a time.

The vast majority of people who say they want to succeed only want to succeed if they can make it all at once. Just one sale won't do it. They want big sales, or thousands of sales, immediately. So, when a new opportunity only produces a few sales, they move on to the next "secret," rather than making those few sales over and over and over and over until those few sales have grown into thousands upon thousands of sales.

Unfortunately, most people are looking for someone to help them do it—or, worse yet, do it for them—rather than looking for the tools they need to do it themselves.

If you want to succeed, *do something*. Let what you are doing lead you onward and upward until you have the success you seek.

There are no "secrets" to it.

Many people know the facts. Many people have the talent. Many people have the need. Many people have what it takes. But very, very few succeed because they are seeking the "secrets" to success rather than doing something to make their success happen.

Over thirty years ago, I coined the phrase "Physio-Psychic Power" to illustrate the methods, techniques, and applications I had used to achieve success in my life and my businesses.

Although I have only occasionally used the phrase in my writings, I have used the premise of "Physio-Psychic Power" as a guide in teaching my methods, techniques and applications of doing business to the over 700 thousand "business people" and "opportunity seekers" who have read my self-published books, booklets, reports and articles.

Over the years, countless of my readers (some of whom have been reading my writings for well over thirty years) have asked me why I didn't put all of my more motivational writings together in one book so they wouldn't have to go digging through their files to find the dog-eared copies they wanted to read again.

When, after much cajoling by one particularly tenacious reader (that's you, Ron), I decided to write this book. Be forewarned, however. I can't tell you any "secrets," but I will tell you some things you probably didn't know yet. You may even re-learn some great truths that you had learned in your youth, but hadn't used or acted upon, simply because they didn't go around disguised as "secrets."

My only hope is that you will enjoy reading and applying "Physio-Psychic Power" as much as I have enjoyed living it and writing about it.

Read it in good wealth.

Now, let's begin to move some mountains…

Mustard Seeds, Shovels, & Mountains

How to Succeed Using Your
Physio-Psychic Power

If ye have faith as a grain of mustard seed, ye shall say unto this mountain, remove hence to yonder place; and it shall remove; and nothing shall be impossible unto you.

—Matthew 17:20

$\mathcal{P}$hysio-$\mathcal{P}$sychic $\mathcal{P}$ower

Over the past fifty-plus years, I have read literally hundreds of books, booklets, manuscripts, reports, and articles on "mind stuff": self-motivation, goal-setting, psychology, philosophy, metaphysics, each and all religions, and even the occult—voodoo, witchcraft, and black magic.

My all time favorite is *The Magic of Believing* by Claude Bristol followed closely by *Think and Grow Rich* by Napoleon Hill along with the writings of W. Clement Stone, Ayn Rand, Norman Vincent Peale, Paul J. Meyer, Mary Baker Eddy, L. Ron Hubbard, Anthony Robbins, Dr. Phil, Oprah, and numerous others.

In my youth, while I was on my own quest for the "secrets" to success, I went through all of the goal-setting, affirmations, visualizations, incantations, prayers, rituals, monotonous repetitions, and mental exercises espoused by each of the methods; even the more esoteric, recondite, abstruse and, sometimes, even ridiculous methodologies, I had read. All the while, I was doing the things I had to do to survive: generate an income and provide for myself and my family.

At times, when my business activities produced some exceptional profits, I firmly believed that the motivational or metaphysical method I was using at the time had caused the abundance, imaging in my young mind that I had indeed found that ever illusive "secret" to success. Then, when my business activities would stabilize without showing any exceptional growth patterns, I would—

again—go in search of the real "secret" of success.

Grabbing another book of "mind stuff," I would again return to my quest for the holy grail of success, all the while doing whatever had to be done to keep generating an income: building my business ever so slowly as I sought the "secret" of success.

Throughout my readings on motivation, religion, metaphysics, mind-power, and even the occult, one statement seemed to be recurring in almost all of the writings. You have, no doubt, seen it quoted (or misquoted) yourself.

"If you have the faith of a mustard seed, you can move mountains."*

One fine day, after having shown no growth in my business activities for some short time, I opened my latest motivational tome to be greeted by that statement. At that moment, not being in an accepting mood, I muttered to myself "Yeah. If you get a shovel and start hauling the mountain away one shovel-full at a time."

That's when it dawned on me that it was my actions, not the goal setting, affirmations, visualizations, incantations, prayers, rituals, repetitions, and mental exercises, that had made my successes possible. It was only when I relied solely upon the incantations, rituals, repetitions, and mental exercises, and quit "doing what needed to be done," that my business stagnated or, in some cases, even lost ground.

When I had "faith" *and* a shovel, I could move mountains; but when I had "faith" without a shovel, the mountain just sat there.

Then, I remembered a sermon I had heard in my youth about "Works Without Faith." The premise of the sermon was that "good works" without "faith" would not get a person into heaven, however, "faith" would, of itself, require "good works" from the holder of the faith.

In other words, even if I had a shovel, I would never move the mountain without the "faith" that I could and would move that mountain.

On the other hand, if I had "faith" that I could and would move that mountain, I would be required by that "faith" to keep getting bigger and stronger shovels to do the job.

---

* The actual Bible verse—Matthew 17:20—is "If ye have faith as a grain of mustard seed, ye shall say unto this mountain, remove hence to yonder place; and it shall remove; and nothing shall be impossible unto you."

That's when I wrote this note to myself.

"Motivation is like a 5-gallon can of gasoline. It won't take you anywhere unless you have a vehicle in which to use it."

Needless to say, after that, I lost my obsession with motivational writings, only reading (more often, *re*-reading) them occasionally in order to reinforce my "faith" in my own ability to move mountains.

A few years later, a young entrepreneur to whom I had given a copy of the book *The Magic of Believing* (when he really needed some "faith" in himself), commented that after reading the book, he had gained the "psychic power" to succeed.

Hearing his comment, I proceeded to explain to him that instead of just psychic power, he needed "physical-psychic power" and told him about my "faith without a shovel" revelation.

Eventually, I shortened my Physical-Psychic Power to "Physio-Psychic Power" and used the premise in all of my books, booklets, reports, and articles to teach my readers how to do the things I had done, interlacing the seeds of "Physio-Psychic Power" in my instructions to inspire the reader to have the "faith" to do what I was teaching.

So, what is "Physio-Psychic Power"?

When combined in application, it goes far beyond the dictionary definitions.

Physio is related to "physical" applications.

Psychic is related to, affected or influenced by the human mind or psyche; mental or even metaphysical.

Power is, of course, the ability or capacity to perform or act effectively; a specific capacity, faculty, or aptitude.

Plainly and simply, *Physio-Psychic Power* is the utilization of physical applications to realize the mental, even metaphysical, manifestations of success.

As we progress, I will endeavor to explain to you the necessary physical actions required to give your "faith" a shovel. At the same time, I will explain how to build your "faith" by using physical applications.

Join me on a new adventure into the power of your mind…

** I have used that statement in a number of my ads over the years.

You must first have the knowledge of your power; second, the courage to dare; third, the faith to do.

—**Charles F. Haanel**

2

Wonders of the Mind

Before we get into the nitty-gritty of using Physio-Psychic Power to get everything you want in life, let's first explain the elements with which we are dealing.

If you have already read some other "mind stuff" writings, you will without doubt be familiar with the terminology being used. Please do me a favor and read my explanations anyway. You might just find a key to understanding that hadn't occurred to you yet.

Everything that you do as a human being requires the combined efforts of both the physical and the mental. Take the simple act of walking across the room as an example. You may not realize it, but walking is a far more complex activity than you might imagine. Walking requires the elements of balance and the coordinated movement of the legs, arms, head, pelvis, torso, and shoulders. When you were an infant, you spent an inordinate amount of time mastering those physical movements. In most cases, however, you were assisted in your attempts by your parents, older siblings, and other relatives and adults. They lifted you up and balanced you on your spindly legs while your brain learned and recorded all of the necessary muscle responses and subtle movements to enable you to balance yourself, stand, and, finally, walk on your own. Today, you walk across the floor with an ease of motion learned from years of practice—a highly complex combination of physical and mental applications.

If you were to sit in a chair and *only think* about walking across the room, you wouldn't move an inch.

On the other hand, if you were to attempt to stand and walk across the room without using your mental faculties, you would move no further than you did by only thinking of walking across the room.

I'm sure I just heard someone say, "Oh, yeah? I can walk without thinking."

Wanna bet? Have you ever watched a drunk try to walk across a room? The physical movement is there, but with the mental faculties impaired by alcohol, the mental coordination of balance and movement of the legs, arms, head, pelvis, torso, and shoulders isn't working in combination with the physical activity. The drunk's head may even flop from side to side as it did before his brain had learned and recorded the physical gyrations necessary to hold the head steady and upright.

Without Physio-Psychic Power—a combination of physical applications learned, recorded, and played back by your sub-conscious mind—you would have never learned to walk.

If you noticed, I just did it. I used that magical, mystical phrase "sub-conscious mind"—that part of your psyche which, according to myth and legend, is capable of producing miracles for you.

Although there has been much written about the "sub-conscious mind" over the past couple centuries, in actuality The sub-conscious mind is *all* mental activity that does not occur in your cognizant conscious mind. That includes all of your memories, experiences, learned applications, and everything else you aren't consciously thinking about right now.

In other words, if you are doing something, but you aren't consciously thinking about it, your sub-conscious mind is simply playing back what it has already learned and recorded as a successful method of achieving your purpose, like walking across the room.

Have you ever been driving your car and realized that you had come a fairly long distance without even realizing it? I have too many times. Your sub-conscious mind was simply playing back what it had already learned and recorded as a successful method of driving a car. You weren't consciously thinking about it, but you were doing it.

On the other hand, if you undertake doing something you

have never done before, it is up to your conscious mind to direct all of your actions. When you finally have that "A-ha! That's the way it's done" moment, your sub-conscious mind faithfully records the requisite actions. When you once again attempt the same undertaking, your sub-conscious mind simply plays back what you have consciously accepted as a successful method of achieving your intended purpose.

It is the same with everything—and I do mean everything—you do throughout your life, whether it be walking across the room or building a mega-billion dollar business. One—either one, physical or mental—without the other will not achieve the desired results.

As an infant, when you first tried to just lift your head, your sub-conscious mind did not say "Contract this muscle this much. Contract that muscle this much. Feel the balancing mechanism in your inner ear? Equalize it. Lift your chin. Now, rotate the cranium forward…." Even at that earliest stage of your development, your conscious mind (as limited as it was) had a desire to peer beyond your flat-on-your-back position. In an attempt to satisfy that desire, your conscious mind sent various signals to the muscles of the neck in an effort to achieve the intended goal. If an effort was unsuccessful in achieving the desired result, that method was discarded and another attempt was made.

When a physical combination of methods was successful in achieving a desired result, that physical application was stored in the sub-conscious mind and was referred to (played back) when called upon to perform the same task again—with the same successful results.

Have you ever noticed that there are some people who go through life with their head tilted ever so slightly to the left or right?

Unless the aberration is caused by some physical deformity, the odds are that during their infancy they had consciously accepted that position of their head as a "successful" attempt at raising their head. Maybe the infant thought it was a successful position because a parent had held the infant's head slightly tilted. In any case, the sequence of physical gyrations that produced what they had consciously accepted as successful was diligently recorded in their sub-conscious mind and each time it becomes necessary for them to lift their head, the same "successful" sequence of physical movements is played back by the sub-conscious mind with the same tilt. That tilted head can be corrected if that person consciously recognizes that their head is tilted and they consciously correct the tilt until they consciously accept it and their sub-conscious plays it back for them.

Such it is with everything we do. Whatever we learn to do and consciously accept as a successful achievement of an intended purpose is recorded in our sub-conscious mind and played back in the same way each time we are called upon to accomplish the same task—even if what is accepted is in error or flawed, as with the slightly tilted head.

On the other hand, if we attempt to learn or do something countless times without success, our sub-conscious mind will faithfully record our lack of success as an "impossible" undertaking, if we consciously accept it as such.

Then again, if we do something that proves to be counter-productive—causing physical harm, loss, pain, humiliation, embarrassment, or fear—our sub-conscious mind may dutifully record the sequence of applications and events as a "caution" against further attempts in the same regard, since taking such action will result in the same consequences. Again, if we consciously accept it as such.

As an example, I remember very vividly that winter day in my youth when I had gone to the kitchen to prepare some hot chocolate. After locating a small sauce pan in which to heat the milk, I went to the cook stove to find a cast iron skillet sitting on the burner I was going to use. Grabbing the handle of the skillet firmly to remove it from the burner, I severely burned the palm of my hand, accompanied by the smell of burning flesh, intense pain, and my screams. My Mother had left the skillet on the burner to cool. To this day, without conscious thought, when I reach for a pan (of any kind) sitting on a stove I instinctively pull back and check to see if it is hot.*

It only took the one time for my sub-conscious mind to record a "caution" against doing that again, which is played back instanta-

---

* I never did get my hot chocolate.

neously each and every time I reach for a pan on the stove.

Other instances where less pain was involved I have (as you have) had to experience physical harm, loss, pain, humiliation, embarrassment, or fear a number of times before the subconscious mind dutifully recorded the "caution" against that specific action.

The sub-conscious mind *does not* at any time, under any circumstance, initiate any activity. Everything and anything you do is first initiated in your conscious mind. If your sub-conscious mind has a pre-recorded instance of that activity that you have consciously accepted as a successful (or unsuccessful) method of achieving your intended purpose, your sub-conscious mind will simply play back that method or caution instantaneously.

For example, just walking across the room requires that your conscious mind initiate the thought of crossing the room. When the conscious command is made, the sub-conscious mind plays back the sequence of actions that must be taken to walk across the room.

What if your sub-conscious mind forgot how to walk or was blocked from remembering how to walk?

Have you ever heard of "psychosomatic paralysis"?

Such psychosomatic paralysis may happen when a person suffers a traumatic shock, either physical or mental. The muscles and nerves are all functioning normally, but, for some unknown reason, the person simply cannot walk.

It could be that the traumatic shock caused the sub-conscious mind to forget how to walk. More likely, something about the traumatic shock caused the person to block the sub-conscious mind from remembering how to walk. In either case, the conscious command to "walk" never reaches the sub-conscious mind and the requisite learned and recorded physical gyrations necessary are not played back.

At the same time, since the sub-conscious mind is nothing more than the repository of everything you have ever heard, said, seen, read, learned, your memories, and all of your life experiences, it sometimes seems to malfunction without cause.

Have you ever tried to answer a question while watching your favorite game show on TV but although you knew you knew the answer you were unable to bring that answer into your conscious mind?

Like you probably have, I have had that experience more times that I can remember. One instance is branded indelibly in my memory.

During my Junior High School years (they call it Middle School now), I was a champion speller. I could spell all of the multi-syllable words on the National Spelling Bee list—even if I didn't know what most of them meant. In the final Spelling Bee to determine who would represent our school in the District Spelling Bee, I was holding my own against my older opponents, spelling every word asked of me.

Then, it happened.

The teacher asked me to spell the word "haul." Without hesitation, I repeated the word "hall," spelled it "H-A-L-L," and repeated the word again, "hall." Whereupon the teacher said, "No. 'Haul.' As in '*Haul* a load of rocks.'"

My mind went blank. All I could think of was "H-A-L-L." I knew it was wrong, but no matter how hard I tried, I could not for the life of me bring the word "haul" into my conscious mind.

Needless to say, I didn't go to the District Spelling Bee and, having been totally embarrassed by my experience, I never competed in any other spelling bees.

You've probably had similar experiences yourself.

On the other hand, what about those times when the answer to almost every question asked seems to just jump into your conscious mind. You even seem to know the answers to questions you didn't even know you knew.

We used to call it being "in the groove." My grandsons say they are "in the zone." No matter what you call it, it is a delightful experience. It's like you can do no wrong. You just seem to know what you need to know without even thinking about it.

How do we sometimes remember things we didn't even know we knew?

Maybe it all relates back to that oft-repeated motivational, metaphysical admonition: "If you have the faith of a mustard seed, you can move mountains."

Which, then, begs the question that will be subject of the next chapter…

$\mathcal{W}$hat $\mathcal{I}$s $\mathcal{F}$aith?

3

Throughout all of the "mind stuff" writings, there is one word common to them all: *Faith.*

What is faith?

If you will look up the word "faith" in your dictionary, you'll find it defined as "Confident belief in the truth, value, or trustworthiness of a person, an idea, or a thing. Belief that does not rest on logical proof or material evidence. Belief, confidence, trust, reliance. Mental acceptance of the truth or actuality of something."

Hmmm...It seems like "belief" is the underlying principle of faith. So, let's go to the dictionary again to learn that "belief" is defined as: "The mental act, condition, or habit of placing trust or confidence in another. Mental acceptance of and conviction in the truth, actuality, or validity of something. Something believed or accepted as true."

Turning to my handy-dandy thesaurus, I find that the only true antonym (that's a word that actually means the opposite) for either "faith" or "belief" is "disbelief." But there are a number of contrasted words (words that aren't really opposites but have nearly-opposite meanings) like "skepticism," "uncertainty," "apprehension," "misgiving," "distrust," "mistrust," "questioning," and "doubt."

When all of those words are looked-up in the dictionary, the one word common to all of them is the word "doubt," which is defined as "To be undecided or skeptical about. To tend to disbelieve;

distrust. To regard as unlikely. To be undecided or skeptical. A lack of trust. A point about which one is uncertain or skeptical. The condition of being unsettled or unresolved."

I'm starting to sound like a bloody English professor, but I'm sure Mrs. Edna Terrell, my high school English teacher, would be proud of me.

By the way, you have just witnessed the physical applications of one of my mental processes. Anytime I am involved in a new undertaking, no matter what it may be, I start with the literal meanings of the words, usually starting with the "glossary" of any book I am reading on the subject (if the book has one). Then I progress to my dictionaries (I have seven of them), followed by the thesaurus, looking up all of the synonyms, antonyms, and relative and contrasted words. I won't even mention my use of grammar, junior high, and high school level encyclopedias. It isn't uncommon for me to sit for hours with a dictionary, thesaurus, and volumes of the encyclopedia in front of me looking up words until I finally understand the subject of my quest.

Anyone can learn the definitions of words, but to gain understanding of those words takes more time and effort than most people want to spend. Yet, it is the *understanding* that leads to accomplishment. If you want to sharpen your mental faculties, I suggest you choose some key words in any undertaking you may choose and follow the same course to understanding.

Returning to my research on the word "faith," by learning the definitions of the word "faith" and the definitions of all the synonyms, antonyms, and relative and contrasted words, we can finally come to the understanding that faith is, in reality, nothing more than an **unquestioning lack of doubt**.

With that understanding, we can change the admonition "If you have the faith of a mustard seed, you can move mountains" to **"If you have an unquestioning lack of doubt, you can move mountains."**

But...but...but...

How do you achieve an unquestioning lack of doubt?

Actually, that's what the goal setting, affirmations, visualizations, incantations, prayers, rituals, repetitions, and mental exercises espoused by each of the various "mind-stuff" methods are supposed to do for you. By following the prescribed systematic procedures, you are supposed to convince your sub-conscious mind that you have faith, believe in your goals, and lack any doubt that what you want is "already yours."

Unfortunately, that's half-right, half-wrong, and backwards.

Beyond that, the vast majority of writings on the subject go so far as to tell you that "the sub-conscious mind doesn't know the difference between the truth and a lie. Once you convince the sub-conscious that what you seek is real, the sub-conscious mind will give it to you."

Your conscious mind does know the difference, though.

As I told you earlier, the sub-conscious mind does *not* at any time, under any circumstance initiate any activity. Everything and anything you do is first initiated in your conscious mind. The sub-conscious mind cannot "give" you anything. Your sub-conscious mind is only a "recording," "play-back," and "internal communications" device.

That being the case, your faith, belief in your goals, and lack of any doubt that what you want can be yours, *must* begin in your conscious mind. Once your conscious mind no longer doubts that you can do or achieve whatever you desire, it is then—and only then—recorded in your sub-conscious mind for later play-back—action, when the necessary "physical" mechanism or opportunity, is in place.

Unless and until your conscious mind accepts your imagined desires are "real," your subconscious mind will not believe and accept them as real no more than your conscious mind does. Your goal setting, affirmations, visualizations, incantations, prayers, rituals, repetitions, and mental exercises only serve to convince yourself—your conscious mind—that what you want can be yours. Once you consciously accept that your goal (whatever it may be) is achievable, it is recorded in your sub-conscious mind and played back with the same acceptance.

In other words, before you convinced yourself—your conscious mind—that your goal was achievable, your sub-conscious mind may have recorded some of your past failures in the same regard and had been playing those instances back as "cautions" against further attempts. Once you have convinced yourself that your goal is achievable, the "doubt" that was already recorded in your sub-conscious mind will be replaced with your new-found "faith."

Thus, the next time the necessary "physical" mechanism, or opportunity, is in place for the accomplishment of your goal, your subconscious will play-back the "faith" you have consciously accepted, without the "doubt" you once had. Removing your "doubt," by consciously accepting that your goal is achievable, can work seeming miracles of faith.

4

$\mathcal{S}$ix $\mathcal{H}$onest $\mathcal{S}$erving $\mathcal{M}$en

$\mathbf{S}$ome of the fondest memories of my youth center around our trips to visit my Dad's sisters and my cousins in Oklahoma, about a three hour drive from where we lived in Kansas. Like so many family outings, the trips were usually made over a weekend, leaving late Friday night or early Saturday morning and returning on Sunday.

One summer, after the wheat harvest was done and the fields were planted with the fall crops, Dad decided to take a one-week vacation from his job at Boeing Aircraft in Wichita, Kansas. We spent that week in Oklahoma visiting, as Dad used to call them, the "in-laws and outlaws."

That particular trip, when I was about twelve years old, sticks in my memory because of the profound lessons I learned that summer.

Never having enough time from my farm chores to do all the fishing I wanted to do, I took my fishing gear with me. While the younger kids played around the house or in the barn, I took my fishing gear and walked down the lane to Cabbage Hollow each morning. Returning each afternoon with a nice stringer of Blue Gill, Crappie, and Catfish, the family enjoyed fresh fish for dinner, after I cleaned and dressed them, of course.

About the third day of my vacation, I happened upon an old man fishing in one of my more productive fishing spots. He nodded to me as I approached and indicated by the wave of a hand that I was welcome to share the spot with him. We fished in silence most of the day except for a brief exchange late in the day when he borrowed my "makin's" to roll himself a cigarette.

That evening, when I mentioned the old man, my Aunt explained that he was a hermit that lived up the other direction in the lane. Nobody knew much about him but he was always ready, willing, and able to lend a helping-hand to anyone in the community when they needed it. He was even known to help-out with cold, hard cash when the situation could only be solved that way. Some said he was an ex-con who had killed a couple of men in Louisiana and spent most of his life in prison, but no one knew for sure. All in all, he was a gentle old man and wouldn't do me any harm.

The next day, the old man was once again fishing in one of my fishing spots. After settling myself in for a day of fishing, the old man proffered his makin's in return for mine from the day before. We struck up a conversation and, as fishermen will do, shared our stories of the big ones we had caught and the ones that got away.

Over the next few days, I learned more than anyone else knew about my new-found fishing friend. Ed was well over 80 years old. When he was a young man, he had been a real riverboat gambler. "Not one of them fancy boys like in the movies," he said. He had never killed anyone that he knew for sure, although he had been in some scrapes with the law when riverboat gambling was being outlawed. (He brought a deck of cards and amazed me with card tricks I had never seen before and haven't figured out to this day.) As riverboat gambling died out, Ed bought a couple of sections of land over by Tulsa. He built a nice home and settled down with his new wife. They soon had a son. Shortly after his son was born, oil was discovered on the property surrounding his. Of course, being a gambler by nature, Ed hired a geologist and drilled a well on his property. That put him in the oil business for about twenty years before he sold out with, in his words, "more money than any man could spend in a lifetime." After selling out, Ed and his wife and son traveled the world visiting all the places he had heard of in his youth. When his son was killed in a boating accident, Ed and his wife retired to Oklahoma City where he dabbled in a number of businesses. When Ed's wife died during the depression, he traveled around the country, never staying very long in any one place, and finally landed in his cabin just above Cabbage Hollow.

During the few days I spent with Ed, the old man shared many lessons with me. Lessons that have proven to be some of the most valuable I ever learned.

Even before Kenny Rogers sang about it, Ed, with a deck of cards between us, taught me when to hold 'em, when to fold 'em, when to walk away, and, the most important lesson, when to "by God, *run!*"

The day before we were to return to Kansas, Ed said he had some very important questions to ask me. It didn't dawn on me until years later just how important those questions were. He asked me, **"Where are you going? Why do you want to go there? What are you going to do when you get there?"**

My youthful answer was that we were going back to Kansas because Dad's vacation time was over. Back to the farm chores. No more fishing.

Ed listened, then said, "That's not what I mean. I want to know where are *you* going?"

That's when he explained to me how important it is in life to *know* where you are going; *know* why you want to go there (nothing happens without a reason); and *know* what you are going to do when you get there. Then, write it down, so you don't forget.

Beyond that, Ed told me to "forget about looking for answers. Learn to ask the right questions. Just remember the words of Rudyard Kipling.

"*I keep six honest serving-men*
"*(They taught me all I knew);*
"*Their names are What and Why and When*
"*And How and Where and Who.*

"Not an answer in the bunch. Just questions. If you ask yourself the right questions, the answers will come to you."

The next time we visited Oklahoma, I learned that Ed had died and was buried in the local cemetery. The whole town was amazed to learn that he had left millions of dollars to charities around the country, including a bequest to the local community to build a community center and ball park for the kids.

Although in my youth I did write down some of my goals— where I was going, why I wanted to go there, and what I wanted to do when I reached those goals—it wasn't until nearly fifteen years later that it dawned on me. Ed had taught me to "set goals," just like all the writers of the "mind stuff" I had read did. The only difference was that Ed included admonitions the others failed to mention.

Beyond just setting a goal, Ed taught me that just as important as the goal was why I wanted to get to my goal and what I was going to do when I had reached that goal.

So, first things first. In your quest…

Where are YOU going?

Why do YOU want to go there?

What are YOU going to do when you get there?

Remember, it is the questions that matter. The answers will manifest themselves when you ask the right questions:

Who? What? Where? When? Why? How?

5

Where Are You Going?

*I*t never ceases to amaze me…Do you realize that the vast majority of people (I hope, not you) really have no idea in the world where they are going? They live their lives doing only what they must do to survive, dreaming of the day they can retire and draw their Social Security benefits. Some of them do a little planning for their retirement years, but fully 90% of them learn too late that their Social Security benefits won't be enough to give them more than a paltry existence. They always thought, "The government will take care of me."*

Many years ago, I told my readers that if they wanted a motivation to achieve some kind of success in their life, they should visit an old folks' home—nursing home, retirement center, whatever—and see if that kind of existence was what they wanted. If nothing else, it will give you a reason to establish some goals in your life.**

Right now, I know someone is saying, "But money isn't everything." I agree whole-heartedly! Goal setting is about succeeding in, accomplishing, or getting everything you want or need throughout your life. It's not necessarily about "money."

---

* It doesn't.

** I quit suggesting that exercise in my writings when I got a number of complaints from the people who run those facilities. They said I was using the inhabitants of those facilities unfairly, that I was maligning those senior citizens for not living a more productive life without knowing the circumstances of their lives. I saw their point and stopped. Then, over the years, I heard from a few of the inhabitants—and they didn't mind me "using them as an example." Still, if you choose to visit one of those "homes," please mind your manners and try not to let-on why you're really there.

Some of the most successful people I know have very little money for money's sake. They have achieved that special state of being exactly where they want to be in life. The goals those people have set for themselves throughout their lives have not involved "money." By achieving their goals, all of their needs are amply provided for without a need for monetary gain.

Mother Theresa is a prime example. Her goals have not involved the accumulation of wealth (money). All of her needs, however, were more than adequately provided. The money she required to accomplish her goals was made available abundantly.

As has been often said, "If money will fix it, it isn't a problem."

No matter what you want from life, you may have it all by simply applying the lesson I learned as a child.

Know where you are going.

Know why you want to go there.

Know what you are going to do when you get there.

Write it down, so you don't forget.

Sounds very much like what every "mind stuff" writer has been saying for years about "goal setting," doesn't it? Then again, it does have a different twist to it.

Until now, you have only been told that you needed to set goals for yourself and write them down using the techniques and methods espoused by your teacher of the moment. Once that has been done, you should bring in the affirmations, visualizations, incantations, prayers, rituals, repetitions, or mental exercises being taught in order for your sub-conscious mind to bring those goals into existence for you (as if it could).

But, nothing happens without a reason. Have you ever read any of the many dissertations on the subject of "cause and effect"? Without a "cause" there can be no "effect" and, although it may be difficult to discern, every "effect" has a "cause."

Your goal, no matter what it may be—monetary, physical, metaphysical, tangible, or intangible—is the "effect" you seek. Without a "cause," it simply can not happen. That is a physical law of nature.

By knowing "why" you want to reach your goal, you can begin applying the *physical law of cause and effect* to your goal—a reason for your goal to be achieved.

Why Mind Stuff Works

6

Without fail, every "mind stuff" writer advises the reader to "set goals," "decide an outcome," "target your objective," or something similar. In many of those writings, the author includes very specific methods for establishing your goals, such as "Should your goal be to have (whatever subject the author is teaching at that moment you should write your goal in this manner." The writer then goes on to explain what words you should use; what words you should avoid; the sequence of those words; how you should breathe before and after re-reading your written goal; any special incantations you should "always" include in your goal; the number and method of repetitions to guarantee your success; any physical gyrations you will need to perform….

Usually, at the end of the dissertation, there are some pre-written goals you can use by simply filling in the blanks with your desires. In some of the occult practices, there are very specific incantations you must use for every specific phenomena, miracle, or marvel, you want to accomplish or create.

Why do they do that?

Those writers know—as I do—that the vast majority of people are just too lazy to really do anything for themselves. So, by including pre-written goals and "specific" instructions, the writer leads the reader to believe that once the pre-written goal is repeated long enough, following the specific instructions, the outcome is assured.

Does it work?

You bet it does—in enough cases to make it a viable methodology.

Why does it work?

Have you ever wondered, as I did for too many years, why every religion has stories of miraculous happenings (miracles) that can be accounted for only by the faith of their followers. It doesn't matter whether the belief was in the teachings of Jesus, Mohammed, Buddha, Ra, Vishnu, Confucius, the Dali Lama, or even Mary Baker Eddy, the miracles happened and have been attributed to the teachings of the specific "master."

As a matter of fact, I mention Mary Baker Eddy specifically because in her writings on "Christian Science," she tells her readers that they don't have to believe what she says. Just read the miraculous stories of those who do believe and the reader will see proof-positive in their own lives, followed by story after story of miraculous cures through prayer without the benefit of medicines.

Miraculously, as the stories of the miracle cures are read, the reader may actually find them self healed of some ailment that had tormented them for years, simply because the reader consciously accepted the premise that such miracles could and would happen. The reader didn't have to "believe" anything. All they had to do was "consciously accept" that it could and would happen to them by reading of the experiences of others who may have shared the same ailment.

Mary Baker Eddy knew—and the "mind stuff" writers and I all know—that once you "consciously accept" that a thing can happen, you will do what is necessary to make it happen, even if what you do isn't consciously done and you may not even be aware that you are doing what you are doing.

In my business writings, I have often been asked about the glowing "testimonials" given for some of the most worthless business ideas, plans, and opportunities. Why would anyone give a glowing testimonial for information that was so clearly and obviously flawed?

Consider this: If only 10% of the information provided by a less-than-totally-knowledgeable business writer/promoter is factual, there will be those among his (or her) readers who will attribute their success to the writer/promoter who awakened the "spirit of success" within them. Those people won't even realize how much they had been mislead until much later, when they look back and compare what they have done to what they had been lead to believe they were supposed to be doing.

To illustrate, let me tell you a true story from my own experience.

Back in my younger days, I made some outrageous money as a finder. Then, in 1978, I created my "Finder's Fee Course," which has since become the bible of that industry, with nearly 70,000 copies sold worldwide. I have very rarely told the story about how that course came into existence.

When I was just a kid growing up on the farm, I discovered that I could make a few extra bucks by putting buyers and sellers together and charging a commission. If farmer Brown had a tractor (or whatever) for sale, I would make an arrangement with him to give me a commission if I could find him a buyer. Then, when I found another farmer who needed such a tractor, I would introduce him to farmer Brown and, if he bought the tractor, I would get my commission. It was easy money because I knew almost everyone in the county, what they had for sale, and what they might buy.

Later, when I was in the Army, I learned that used car salesmen would pay me what they called a "bird dog fee" if GIs I brought to their lots bought a car. Again, I was earning finder's fees, by introducing buyers to sellers, but I didn't know it at the time.

Sometime during my stint in the Army, I somehow acquired an old book about unusual businesses. In that book, there was a rather lengthy chapter about earning finder's fees. That chapter mentioned that finder's fees could be earned in the fields of industrial and oil field equipment (just like farm tractors), close-outs, liquidations, collectibles, and a whole world of areas I had never even considered.

Even before I got out of the Army, I had started earning bigger and bigger finder's fees on all kinds of products and services just by introducing buyers to sellers as I had "learned" in that old book. By the mid-1970s, I was known internationally as a successful finder, earning some outrageous fees for finding some of the most diverse products and services you can imagine.

For well over 10 years, I firmly believed that my success as a finder was due to what I had learned from that single chapter in the old book I had read. And, had anyone ever asked, I would have "testified" that I owed my success to that author.

As I pursued my career as a finder, I read everything I could find about finder's fees. Everything I read was bulls—...You know the rest of that word. None of it even vaguely resembled the "truth" about being a finder and when I was able to actually speak to the authors, I learned that they, personally, had never earned any finder's fees, but they had read about it. (Maybe in the same book I had read.)

In 1978, when I decided to teach people how to really and truly earn finder's fees, I went back into my archives and retrieved the old book I had read, thinking I would use the chapter on finder's fees in it to start my course. Guess what? Re-reading the chapter on finder's fees in that old book, I learned that what the author had written was actually even more misleading than the pure bulls— I had read since. (It's a good thing I had never given the author a testimonial.) But, something in that book had inspired me to decide to expand my activities as a finder.

So, you see, even though only 10% of the information provided by a "mind stuff" writer may be viable, there will be those among his (or her) readers who will find within themselves the inspiration to succeed and achieve their goals. Those few will give glowing testimonials to the efficacy of the writer's teachings, fully believing that the information that writer provided was instrumental in their success, not realizing that it was their own thinking that produced the results. Once those people had made the decision to succeed, it matters not that over 90% of what they have read is worthless. They will, as I did in my pursuit of finder's fees, adapt, adopt, develop, and implement the methods necessary to achieve their success.

Once the decision is made, you will do it! Your decision *must* come first. As Ben Stein said, "The indispensable first step to getting the things you want out of life is this: decide what you want."

The same holds true for any goal you might establish for yourself. **You *must* decide exactly what you really want.**

It really doesn't matter what inspires you to make that decision. Whether the information you are relying upon is the best, most reliable and factual dissertation ever written on the subject, or pure bulls—, your decision to do it, no matter what it is you decide to do, will produce the results you anticipate and expect.

Think about it! Relate your decision making to anything (and everything) in your life. When you are indecisive, you wander around in a state of perplexity. Nothing seems to go right. Then, when a decision (about anything) is finally made, the stress is relieved and you can go on about whatever you are doing and accomplish your intended goal. Even if the decision is to give-up or quit or just forget it, the result is the same: You do it!

When *you* finally and unequivocally decide that you are going to succeed at something —anything—you will do it. That's why all of the great teachers of "mind stuff" emphasize goal setting. Once you decide upon a goal, you will find a way—even though you stumble and fall along the way to get to that goal. The decision to get to your goal is all it takes!

The decision is yours and yours alone! In the words of Galileo: "You cannot teach a man anything; you can only help him to find it within himself."

So, it isn't who you believe, it is *what you consciously accept* that will make your goals a possibility. If you cannot or will not "consciously accept" that you can do a thing, all the facts in the world will not sway you from your "conscious decision" that it will not work for you.

When I set goals for myself, I use the methodology taught me on the creek bank in Cabbage Hollow when I was but a lad. By following a similar path, you may also establish your goals.

Know where you are going.
Know why you want to go there.
Know what you are going to do when you get there.
Write it down, so you don't forget.

The man who is certain to advance is the one who is too big for his place, and who has a clear concept of what he wants to be; who knows that he can become what he wants to be and who is determined to be what he wants to be.

—Wallace D. Wattles

7

Make a Road Map to Your Goal

As in the physical world of travel, you may not need a road map to get to where you're going. From anywhere in the continental U.S., you can finally get to California by simply heading west. If you, by chance, end up in Oregon or Washington, all you gotta do from there is head south. Before too long, you'll be in California.

The very same holds true for every "general" goal you may have. What if you want to take a vacation to a *specific* location in California?

You can just head west and, eventually, get to California, but to find that specific location in California could take forever without a road map or a friendly mentor to point you in the right directions. (California is a big place.)

So, before you begin establishing your goals, you must…

Know where you are going.

First, you will need a *general goal* in order to establish the direction in which you must start your quest. Then, you will need *specific goals* ("landmarks") along the way so you will know when you are getting closer to your destination.

Did I just hear someone say, "I ain't going anywhere, but there are some things I want and some things I want to do."

Where you are "going" is your "goal," be it person, place, or thing; physical or metaphysical; tangible or intangible; paper, scissors, or rock; meat, fruit, or vegetable; *whatever* your goal may be.

As simple as it sounds, the vast majority of people have no idea in the world where they are going. They just travel life's road doing only what must be done in order to have something to eat, a place to live, clothing to wear, and a mode of transportation. Even the "homeless" share those same goals, albeit on a daily basis.

Every once in a while, those people dream of what it would be like to have or do something, but their dreams are only a fanciful respite from their everyday, mundane existence. They do nothing to make their dreams a reality, but thoroughly enjoy their fantasy vacations from their lives.

In the physical world, if you were planning a vacation trip to a specific location in California, you would probably get a flat map of the continental U.S. and begin by marking on that map your current location. Then, you would mark your specific destination.

Back when I used to do it that way, after I marked my "starting point" and my "final destination," I would take a straight-edge ruler and draw a straight line between those points. Then, I would select the highways that ran as close to that line as possible to get me from here to there.*

Unfortunately, in life there is no single big map upon which you can mark your "starting point" and your "final destination." As a matter of fact, there are so many twists and turns in anyone's life's journey, the only absolute you will have is your "starting point." From there, your "final destination" may change many times as you encounter unforeseen obstacles or exceptional fortuities. Along the way, you may even find a place that gives you all the happiness, sense of achievement, fulfillment, joy, and pleasure you had envisioned to be only at your "final destination." Thus, your goal will have been achieved without completing the journey you had originally intended.

Let's pretend for a moment that your goal is to find and marry

---

* Not wanting to deviate too much from my straight line, I sometimes found myself on some of the most god-awful roads on my way to my final destination. Same thing in some other of my life's journeys.

your soul mate. You choose a specific target: that lovely lady who works in the office down the hall. Although you have made that lovely lady your goal (final destination), what if, on your quest to gain her affection, you encounter another lovely lady along the way, a picture of perfection who sweeps you off your feet, wins your heart, satisfies your every need, and drives thoughts of the first lovely lady from your conscious mind. Would you be wise to continue to pursue your original goal or accept a superior final destination who offered you all the happiness, sense of achievement, fulfillment, joy, and pleasure you had envisioned to be only at your envisioned final destination?

Sounds silly, doesn't it?

But, believe it or don't, there are all too many people who would forsake the second lovely lady and trudge onward on their quest for their original goal simply because that was their intended goal and nothing less would do. Those are the same people who find that, when they have reached their original goal, she turns out to be a witch[**].

That's why, on your life's journey, you need both a general goal and intermediate specific goals to bring you to your final destination.[***]

Returning to our example of your love life, had you established a goal (final destination) of "a soul mate; a picture of perfection, who would sweep you off your feet, win your heart, and satisfy your every need," you would have established a viable "general goal."

With an intermediate goal of "that lovely lady who works in the office down the hall," you would have begun your quest, perfected your approach, honed your abilities, enhanced your appearance, and gained the self-confidence you needed to court that lovely lady.

Even if you never encountered the lovely lady of your intentions, the preparations you made in pursuit of your goal would have

---

[**] Spelled with a capital "B."

[***] A note to the female readers: You will have to forgive me. I am noticeably of the male persuasion. Therefore, throughout my writings you will have to endure my use of male perspective. For me to even *attempt* to fathom the female perspective would be the height of arrogant audacity. Any man who claims otherwise is either a fool or a liar. I only use the female perspective when I am referring to a specific female within my knowledge. Thank you kindly for understanding.

enabled you to reach your "final destination" when you met the lovely lady who offered you all the happiness, sense of achievement, fulfillment, joy, and pleasure that you had envisioned.

So, before you begin establishing any goals, you must answer the question **Where you are going?**

Betcha don't know. Most people don't.

As I said before, most people just travel life's road doing only what must be done in order to have something to eat, a place to live, clothing to wear, and a mode of transportation. That being said, most of them do have a final, general goal: to retire, draw their Social Security benefits, and do nothing until they die. Then, they want to leave a healthy life insurance benefit for their offspring.[****]

Even though those people have no real idea of "where" they are going, they do have a general sense of where they will be at life's end. To that end, they do what must be done—establishing intermediate goals: to have something to eat, a place to live, clothing to wear, and a mode of transportation, with a little left over to pay the life insurance premiums each day.

Why do they live their lives like that?

Simple. That's the way their parents live, their grandparents lived, their siblings, uncles, aunts, cousins, and everyone they know live. They have unconsciously accepted their "fate" (final goal) without question. These people will never leave their mundane existence until they consciously accept the fact that they can have, be, or do anything beyond what they have consciously accepted as their "fate."

One Sunday afternoon, while I was napping in my easy chair, my wife tuned-in to a made-for-TV movie[*****] about a young girl, the daughter of drug addicts who was living on the streets. Upon the death of her drug-addicted mother, she looked around at the people attending the pauper's funeral and decided that that was *not* the way she wanted to end her life. At that point she made a conscious decision to be more than what she had for a heritage. Even though her "friends" ridiculed her, she went back to high school

---

[****] Some of their offspring have the general goal of waiting for the old folks to die so they can collect the proceeds of the life insurance policies.

[*****] *Homeless to Harvard: The Liz Murray Story.*

while living on the streets and in the subway while she attended classes with classmates two to three years her junior. Finishing high school in only two years, she applied for and received a special education grant and was accepted into Harvard University with enough grant money to afford a place to live and clothes to wear.

There was a lot more to the story, but had she not consciously accepted that she could be more than what her heritage had allowed, she would, no doubt, still be living on the streets with her friends and family.

Although the movie interrupted my Sunday afternoon nap, it was a joy to watch as the young lady made her general goal to be more than what her heritage had allowed, established her intermediate goals, and overcame the obstacles of life as she moved ever forward toward that goal.

Unfortunately, even most people who read "mind stuff" writings satisfy themselves with the establishment of intermediate goals only. They set goals to gain a new position in life, acquire physical possessions, accomplish feats of physical or mental prowess, receive a certain monetary amount, or achieve something they envision as "nice to have," but they still have no idea where the achievement of those intermediate goals will take them on their life's journey.

Take as an example the young man who, being a car-nut, establishes the goal of "owing a Rolls Royce." Fine and dandy, but where will it take him on his life's journey?

I think I just heard someone say, "It'll take him anywhere he wants to drive it." That may be so, but I wonder that if "owning a Rolls Royce" is his final goal, then what next? Will he end up being "that bum who owns a Rolls."

I once knew a real bum who drove the shiniest Packard sedan in town. He worked at menial jobs, barely had enough to eat, lived wherever he could off the charity of the churches, spent hours each day waxing and shining his Packard, but was the joke of the town when he drove down Main Street. He died happy, in poverty, and his beloved shiny Packard was sold to pay his funeral expenses.

Maybe back when he decided upon his goal of owing a Packard sedan, he said to himself, "I can die happy, if I own a Packard sedan." Nothing else mattered to him. But, imagine the kind of resolve it took for him to acquire that Packard in the first place. It was one of the most expensive cars on the road back then. Had his life's goal been more than just "dying happy owing a Packard sedan," who knows what he might have accomplished during his lifetime.

As someone once said, "Beware of what you wish for...you just might get it!"

If you know where you are going, your intermediate goals take on a special significance. Each new intermediate goal is just another landmark on the road to your chosen destiny.

Back when I was a young man, the rich oil men would drive up in their big Cadillacs and ask, "Hey, boy. Do you know how I can get to so-and-so's place?" Then, they would spin dirt on me as they drove off in a hurry to get to where they were going.

My first reaction was, "Go ahead. Spin dirt on me. One of these days I'll own a Cadillac, too." Then, it dawned on me. I didn't just want the Cadillac, I wanted to be rich, **rich, rich**—and never spin dirt on anyone like they had. To this day, I drive Cadillacs. They ain't much anymore, just another sardine can with a fancy emblem on the hood, but I still drive a Cadillac—and I never spin dirt on anyone.

Where are *you* going?

Before you set goals to gain a new position in life, acquire physical possessions, accomplish feats of physical or mental prowess, receive a certain monetary amount, or achieve something you envision as "nice to have," *decide what your final destination will be.* Whether your final destination is to be another Mother Theresa or another Bill Gates or somewhere in between or to just be more than what your heritage would allow, figure out where you are going. Once you have made that decision—and consciously accept the fact that you can get there—your intermediate goals will take you where you intend going.

Of course, beyond determining where you are going, you need to ask yourself...

Why do *you* want to go there?

What are *you* going to do when you get there?

When I made the decision that I wanted to be rich, **rich, rich** like the oil men who had spun dirt on me, "why" I wanted to be rich was only in retaliation for the perceived offense against me for not being rich. A few years later, I found a rational reason why I wanted to be rich.

In the small town in Kansas where I grew up—population 1,000, counting some cats and dogs—the school sponsored lyceums. Each of us paid a dime (10¢) to hear or see a special presentation in the school auditorium. Some of the ones I remember were a magician, a juggler, an acrobatic troupe, a ping-pong team from China, a Filipino telling us about the Philippines, and a demolition expert setting off small dynamite blasts on the baseball field. The one who gave me a "why" for my goal was a Catholic priest.

Since our town was predominantly Protestant with a small group of older, retired Jews and only one Catholic family (that I knew of), the priest went into great detail about the priesthood. He explained some of their teachings and the vows they took upon becoming priests.

That evening, my Dad must have sensed that I was perplexed and asked me what was bothering me. I explained that a Catholic priest had spoken at school that day and I just couldn't figure out why anyone would want to take a vow of poverty. Being poor was bad enough without vowing to be that way. As always, Dad had an answer.

"Son, they take a vow of poverty because they honestly believe that they can help poor people by being one of them; but if you really want to help people, get rich. A rich man can help more people in a day than a poor man can help in a lifetime."

Dad may not have been entirely right in his assessment of the priest's vow of poverty, but he wasn't wrong either. A rich man *can* help more people in a day than a poor man can help in a lifetime. In any case, my Dad's homespun logic gave me a "why" for my decision to become rich. It also set for me a goal for what I was going to do once I got rich.

It may well be that your ultimate goal isn't quite as exuberant as mine, but in the preparation of your goal, you must know "why" you want to achieve that goal.

Suppose your ultimate goal is to have a bigger house. Your "why" might be because you've just had another child and want more space; or you just want room to have a workshop, a library, or an extra bedroom for guests. It doesn't matter, as long as you know "why" you want it.

When you get that bigger house, you may decide that you will be able to give your kids a better neighborhood in which to grow up; grow a little (or maybe a big) garden to have fresh veggies; or whatever.

Once you have decided to get a bigger house, know "why" you want it and "what" you are going to do when you have it—*and consciously accepted that you can and will have a bigger house.* You can, then, begin generating your intermediate goals in order to achieve your ultimate goal of a bigger house.

Your first intermediate goal will, of course, be to find the house you want.

Easy enough. Just start looking! Answer real estate ads. Talk with a broker. Drive around the neighborhoods in which you would like to live. The "psychic" part—consciously accepting that you will have a bigger house—has already been done. Now, you have to do the "physical" part by getting off your backside and finding the house you want.

No matter how many affirmations, visualizations, incantations, prayers, rituals, repetitions, or mental exercises you may employ, the house you want isn't going to walk up and introduce itself to you. You gotta go find it.

If you don't know where you are going, why you want to go there, and what you are going to do when you get there, your journey will never begin. Remember, it is the *questions* that matter. The answers will manifest themselves when you ask the right questions.

Who?

What?

Where?

When?

Why?

How?

8

If You Don't Know Where You're Going...

If you don't know where you're going, how will you know when you get there. It might be somewhere else!

What was the first job you ever had? I don't mean mowing lawns, raking leaves, baby-sitting, shoveling snow, delivering newspapers, or selling Christmas cards. Those are actually small businesses. I mean a job where you got a payroll check from your employer for working for them.

Most people—even me—got their first payroll job by answering the "Help Wanted" ads in the newspaper, going from business to business filling out applications, hearing about a "job opening" from a friend or relative, or (like some people) just joining the military. Actually, my first payroll job was an accident and I didn't even know it was a payroll job.

When I was about sixteen years old, during the summer I ran hay-hauling crews for farmers around the county. I hired the boys to haul the hay, charged 12¢ per bale to load, haul and stack the hay, and paid the boys a total of 9¢ per bale among them. From the 3¢ per bale, I paid rent for the trucks and loaders (if the farmer couldn't provide them), gas for the trucks, meals for the crews, and (usually) had about 1¢ per bale profit for my efforts. The hay fields we worked usually produced from 1,000 to 20,000 bales and I had three crews working at most times loading, hauling, and stacking from 1,000 to 1,400 bales per day per crew. I made from $70 to $80 per day when we worked, depending on the weather and field growth. That was at a time when most grown men were earning from $40 to $50 per week salary!

That particular summer was a wet summer. It rained almost every day. When the fields are wet, you can't mow, rake, or bale hay. So, by and large, we sat on our hands waiting for at least a week of dry weather, which were few and far between.

During one of those wet spells, a friend of mine mentioned that the grain elevator was hiring men to unload boxcars filled with bagged fertilizer and stack those bags in their warehouse areas. I knew I wouldn't make the kind of money I made hauling hay, but it was inside and I could pick up some money while it was raining. I took some of my crew with me.

After four long days of unloading and stacking literally thousands of 50-pound bags of fertilizer, all the boxcars were unloaded. When I went to the office to collect my money (about $14, if memory serves), they asked for my Social Security Number. I didn't have one and didn't even know what it was. Neither did most of my crew. The boss man couldn't pay us without it. Whereupon we all went to the local Post Office where we filled out the form.

About a week later, my Social Security Number arrived in the mail and I collected my first payroll check. (Sometimes I wish I had forgotten about the $14 and never got that number.) I had taken that job without knowing it was a "payroll job" for the sole purpose of making a few bucks until the weather permitted me to put my crews back to work.

Later in life, I held a number of jobs. Most of them were taken for the purpose of just keeping body and soul together or to keep my wife and kids fed and clothed while I pursued my fledgling business interests.

When most people start out on their life's journey, their general goal is to "get a job." The purpose of that job is to have something to eat, a place to live, clothing to wear, and a mode of transportation. To that end, they will take just about any job that happens to be available.

The vast majority of people just move from job to job, never wondering—or even imagining—where that job might take them.

As long as the job will provide them with the means to get something to eat, a place to live, clothing to wear, and a mode of transportation, that job serves its purpose. Most people move on from their first job to a "better" job...then a "better" job than that...then another and another. At some point in their "job hopping," they find a job where they can live comfortably—or at least pay all of their bills—at the level of society they have chosen for themselves. They really don't know where they are going, but they are sure to get there.

Other people hold a variety of jobs while they attend college or a trade school. Upon graduation, they focus their job hunting on the subject of their studies or academic discipline. Again, they take a job until they can move on to a better job in the same field...then another and another...until they find *the* job that satisfies their ambitions (large or small). Although they don't know where they are going either, at least those people have established "what" they want to do. Unfortunately, the vast majority of college and trade school graduates never find employment in their field of study and begin their job-hopping career just as they would have without paying for all that education.

Then again, some people establish what they want to do from the very first job they take. In that job they find something that interests them and drives them onward and upward to the pinnacle of success in that field. It can happen in any job, no matter how lowly or menial.

I think I just heard someone say, "Oh, yeah? How can a job flippin' burgers at McDonalds lead onward and upward to the pinnacle of success?"

Well, have you ever read the story of Dave Thomas, the founder of Wendy's restaurants? According to the stories I have read, Dave's first job was as a fry-cook at a fast food restaurant. He enjoyed the work and the food service business. From there, he moved on to "better" jobs in the industry. He had found "what" he wanted to do. Somewhere along the line, Dave Thomas decided—*made a goal*—to own a restaurant of his own. Then, a chain of restaurants. Leading to the founding of the Wendy's restaurants we all know and enjoy when we want to know "Where's the beef?"

By the way, some years ago, I was approached by two different individuals seeking financing to buy a fast food restaurant franchise. Neither of them had any experience in the field or any real business experience, but had read of the fortunes to be made. Beyond that, neither of them had the credit (or rich relatives) to obtain the financing to purchase the franchise they wanted. I gave both of them the same advice: Take a job in one of the franchise restaurants, even if it was just sweeping up out back, to begin with. Work diligently. Perform every task asked of you. If you can, move on to better and better jobs in that restaurant. If you can't move up in that restaurant, find a job at another restaurant. Eventually, move into a management position with that franchise restaurant. At that point you will be in a better position to seek financing to purchase a franchise restaurant of your own through a bank, the franchise owner for whom you are working, or the franchisor itself.

One of the fellows let me know in no uncertain terms that he wasn't going to "take any job flippin' burgers" and move up to management. It could take ten years to do that and he wanted a franchise now, not ten years from now! Five years later he unknowingly submitted the same loan proposal to me seeking financing to buy a fast food franchise restaurant. He had done nothing to gain any experience in the field he had chosen and was still working at the same job he had five years before.

The other fellow thanked me for my advice. He said he would do it because he really wanted to own a fast food franchise restaurant. I didn't hear anything from him for two years.

Two years later, I happened to meet that young man at a business seminar where I was speaking. After introducing himself and thanking me again for the advice I had given him, he told me his story.

After hearing my advice, he had quit his job and taken a job (at much less pay) in a franchised fast food restaurant like the one he wanted to own. Within six months, he had moved up to the position of assistant manager. Three months later, the owner of the restaurant was ready to open a second franchised fast food restaurant and asked the young man to be the manager of that restaurant. Within six months, after fully training two very competent assistant managers, he approached the franchise owner about getting a franchise of his own. To make a long story short, the franchise owner made him a partner and they bought another franchise together. When I met him, the young man was negotiating to buyout his partner and was making plans to buy another franchise of his own.*

No matter what your goal may be, whether it be for a soul mate, a new car, a bigger house, a fortune, or whatever, *once you know where you are going and decide to go there, you will find a way—if you pursue it.* Any affirmations, visualizations, incantations, prayers, rituals, repetitions, or mental exercises you employ will only serve to keep you focused—as long as you know where you are going.

Throughout your life's journey, have a purpose for every endeavor you undertake, whether it be just to keep body and soul together, support your family, further your career, or keep your fledgling business operating. Without a purpose, you'll be like a ship without a rudder: you'll be going somewhere, but you won't know where until you get there.

You can't get to where you *want* to be unless you ask…

Who? What? Where? When? Why? How?

---

* After writing that, I contacted the young man (he ain't so young anymore; then again, neither am I) to find out how it went from there. Today, he owns *seven* franchised fast food restaurants, three of them with another franchisor, effectively competing with himself in two markets.

Those who have cultivated the habit of persistence seem to enjoy insurance against failure. No matter how many times they are defeated, they finally arrive up toward the top of the ladder.

—**Napoleon Hill**

9

$\mathcal{T}$he $\mathcal{P}$assion $\mathcal{P}$it

When I began writing this tome of what I hope that you find to be inestimable wisdom, I went back into my archives and seriously reviewed all of the "mind-stuff" books I have—about two hundred of them all together.

Throughout those books, one admonition seems to prevail. Some of them even insist that it is the *most important* element in the achievement of your goals!

If you are going to achieve your goals, you need to have a burning, all-consuming, passionate, obsessive desire to achieve that goal. Then, your sub-conscious mind will make it happen for you. Some of the writers even go so far as to give instructions about how to create a burning, all-consuming, passionate, obsessive desire with all of the necessary and required affirmations, visualizations, incantations, prayers, rituals, repetitions, or mental exercises to employ.

Wait a minute! What if your burning, all-consuming, passionate, obsessive desire was to have that pretty lady in the office down the hall as your soul mate? Could—or would—any of your affirmations, visualizations, incantations, prayers, rituals, repetitions, or mental exercises (fantasies) create within that pretty lady the same feelings?

I think not!

A burning, all-consuming, passionate, obsessive desire is

neither necessary *nor* required in order to have anything—or everything—you want from life. As a matter of fact, such an all-consuming desire may well drive you to do things which may be counterproductive in other areas of your life.

In the case of money-making goals, a burning, all-consuming, passionate, obsessive desire could lead a person to commit fraud, steal, swindle, or embezzle in order to reach their money goal. How about the man who has such a burning, all-consuming, passionate, obsessive desire to have a certain woman that he becomes a stalker? Or worse yet, a rapist!

A burning, all-consuming, passionate, obsessive desire is really *not* that important to the achievement of your goals.

Rather than working yourself into a frenzy trying to create a burning, all-consuming, passionate, obsessive desire for what you want, *simply decide what you want.* Then, think about it until you can consciously accept the fact that you can get it.

Believe it or don't, during my fifty-plus years in business, not once have I had a burning, all-consuming, passionate, obsessive desire to make money or get rich. All I have ever had was a "reason" I wanted to make money or get rich.

Sometimes, back in the beginning, my reason was as simple as keeping myself fed and clothed. Other times, my reason was to keep my wife and kids fed and clothed; get enough extra money to buy inventory or advertising for my fledgling business; provide better products or services for my customers; fulfill a need expressed by my customers; or provide a product or service needed, but lacking, in our society. There was no burning, all-consuming, passionate, obsessive desire about it.

Once I had decided what I wanted or needed to do, I watched, listened, read, and studied what others with similar ideas were doing. Then, when I had consciously accepted the fact that I could do it, I just went ahead and did it.

Back in my younger days, I even did some things for the same reason Sir Edmund Hillary climbed Mount Everest. Simply because "it was there."

Watching acrobats walking a tightrope, motorcyclists riding round and round on the inside of a big barrel, weight lifters bench pressing more than twice their physical weight, race car drivers zooming around the track at speeds in excess of 180 miles per hour.... I, at first, doubted I could do it. Then it dawned on me that if another living, breathing human being could do it, so could I.[*] Once I decided I wanted to do it and consciously accepted the fact that I could do it, I did it.

Look around you. Is there another living, breathing human being doing what you want or need to do? If some other living, breathing human being can do it, so can you and you won't need a burning, all-consuming, passionate, obsessive desire to do it, either.

That even applies to people with physical handicaps.

I wouldn't necessarily tell a paraplegic person they could ride a bicycle, but I know of such a person who does amazing things on a hand-pedaled bicycle.

All you really need to do is answer the questions.

Where are you going?

Decide what you want to do. Then watch, listen, read, and study what others with similar ideas are doing. If some other living, breathing human being can do it, so can you.

Once you have consciously accepted the fact that you can do it, you will. But, you must know...

Why do you want to go there?

Without a reason, even if your reason is simply the same as Sir Edmund Hillary's "because it is there," you will never do it, even if you consciously accept the fact that you can do it.

A wide gulf exists between knowing that you *can* do it and doing it. The answers are always in the questions you ask yourself.

Who?

  What?

    Where?

      When?

        Why?

          How?

---

[*] Yes, I did all of those things back in my wayward youth. No, I wouldn't want to try it today. Although, with the right personal incentives, I probably could.

Almost everything—all external expectations, all pride, all fear of embarrassment or failure—these things just fall away in the face of death, leaving only what is truly important. Remembering that you are going to die is the best way I know to avoid the trap of thinking you have something to lose. You are already naked. There is no reason not to follow your heart.

—Steve Jobs

10

How to Get Everything You Want

Many years ago, when I was the editor/ publisher of America's leading business opportunities newsletter, a fellow by the name of Carlton Sheets sent me a review copy of his new *No Money Down* real estate course. Recently, after watching one of Carlton's late-night infomercials, I bought his latest course with all the books, CDs, and videos. After all these years, Carlton's course still teaches the same exceptionally effective methods for acquiring real estate as it did nearly thirty years ago, the only real difference being the teaching tools employed. But...

There have been countless articles written and postings to Internet real estate forums and discussion boards decrying Carlton's course as a rip-off, stating emphatically that it "can't be done." In other words, the writers of those articles and postings couldn't, wouldn't, or just didn't do it.

Counter to those negative "it can't be done" articles and postings, there are a host of articles and postings giving testimony to the fact that Carlton's teachings are do-able. A great many of them tell of their own experiences using those teachings to generate some absolutely amazing profits.*

---

* By the way, I have done it myself. My wife Delores and I purchased a $500,000

Why then are there opposing views?

The answer is simple: Once Carlton has taught you "how" you can do it and you have consciously accepted the fact that it can be done, you will have the personal courage to *ask* for the alternative financing methods that Carlton has taught you. Those who fail with Carlton's course never truly consciously accept the fact that it can be done so they never ask, usually because they have read somewhere or someone told them that "it can't be done."

Actually, the only thing Carlton's course teaches you is *what* to ask for and *how* to ask for it. Hopefully, that will instill in you the courage to ask.

If you have read any of my business writings over the past 37 years, you may have noticed that I have CAPITALIZED, *italicized*, <u>underlined</u> or **emboldened** one word almost every time I have used it. That word is **ASK**.

Whether your goal is to have that pretty lady in the office down the hall as your soul mate or to have a million dollars...***All you gotta do is ask!***

If your goal is to have that pretty lady in the office down the hall as your soul mate, how far do you think you'll get if you don't *ask* her out?

Should your goal be a bigger or better house, you **ask** by looking, answering real estate ads, talking with a broker, driving around the neighborhoods in which you would like to live. The **ask**ing doesn't necessarily mean posing the question to anyone. It can be any method of inquiring.

The same holds true even if your goal is to "make a million dollars." You <u>ask</u> by inquiring into the methods and applications employed to "make money."

Let me ask you a question.

Are you stupid?

Thankfully, almost no one is stupid about *everything*. Then again, unfortunately, almost everyone is stupid about some things.

Do you ask questions about the things you want to know

---

home with no money down and we put over $5,000 in our pocket at closing. In another case fifteen years before that, I acquired a $200,000 office building for an out-of-pocket payment of $800. So, I know for a fact that it can be done.

about? Or do you just accept whatever answers you can find on your own, not wanting to appear to be stupid?

When you are asked a question, do you respond by quoting, almost word for word, the answer given by some authority figure (or, worse yet, the party-line) without thinking?

Do you ever question the answers you already think you know? I do—all the time.

When faced with two answers to the same question, do you *ask* yourself *why* there are two answers? Do you ever *ask* yourself whether or not the person giving you an answer has an ulterior motive?

Fortunately, all you have to do is ASK!

Stupidity can be cured!

Every condition in your life has it's cause. Poor people are poor because they have never *ask*ed themselves "Why am I poor?" They just accept the condition and pass it along to their offspring.

Unless you learn to ask for what you want from life, you will be stupid. But, you have to keep on *asking* and *asking* and *asking* until you get the answers that will, finally and lastingly, lead you to a full understanding of success in business and in life.

Ask and you will receive. It is better to appear to be stupid in the eyes of really stupid people than to not ask and *really* be stupid yourself.

"You gotta ask" is also another way of saying "You must advertise."

To achieve their goals—more customers—businesses advertise by **ask**ing you to visit their store or buy their products or services by "advertising" their location and/or availability.

When you *ask*, you are, in effect, "advertising" for what you need to accomplish your goal, whether it be a date with that pretty lady in the office down the hall, a bigger, better house, or even a million dollars.

As a matter of fact, you can literally "advertise" for anything you want!

Some time ago, while browsing the classified ads on the Internet, I came across an ad that read "How can I make money?" with an e-mail address to which I could respond. Responding to the ad, I advised the advertiser that I had made money in a wide variety of businesses and had written step-by-step, detailed reports about how I had done it. I gave him the URL to my catalog page where he could find information about the businesses I had written about. She eventually bought a half-dozen of my reports, manuals, and courses on doing business.

Looking for a soul mate? Today you can even "advertise" for possible soul mates through a wide variety of dating services, both online and off-line.

No matter what your goal, ambition, aspiration, desire, objective, intention, or purpose, you can "advertise"—ASK—for it or how to get it. **You can have anything and everything you want from life if you just *ask*.** Of course, the questions you must *ask* are...

Who? What? Where? When? Why? How?

11

*F*ailure *???*

A few chapters ago, I told you about the mental "mishap" I had when I was competing in a spelling bee. It was the District Spelling Bee and I was asked to spell the word "haul." That's when my mind went blank and all I could think of was "H-A-L-L." No matter how hard I tried I could not bring the word "haul" into my conscious mind. I revisit this story to pose a simple question:

Why do we sometimes forget the things we know we know?

Many—even most—of the mind-stuff writers would immediately label it "fear of failure." In actuality, it is far less sinister.

At that moment during the spelling bee, my mind was preoccupied with unrestrained thoughts of my embarrassment. I did not *fear* failure. My mind was so involved with my thoughts of *embarrassment* that it couldn't think of how the word should be spelled

Unlike a computer that can run a number of applications at once, the human mind is incapable of holding more than one thought at a time. So, while my mind was preoccupied with thoughts of my embarrassment, my mind was unable to bring the word "haul" into my conscious mind.

If you don't believe it, try this…

Re-read the last paragraph aloud and at the same time divide 2,286 by 127. You can't do it. Either you will stop reading and do the math problem or you will stop doing the math problem in order to keep reading. You will not be able to do both at the same time.

It is the same with your goals.

When you let thoughts of the things you will have to give up in order to achieve your goal, your mind is preoccupied with thoughts of all you might lose. **Whether you want to accept it or not, everything in life has its price—something you must lose or give up in order to obtain it.**

If you haven't, yet, gained success, look around you. What are you protecting? If you lost it all tomorrow, would you really lose anything of great value?

People fail not because they cannot succeed, but because they are unwilling to risk what they have. They "protect" their mediocrity until it is all they have left. They are so wrapped-up in "protecting" and "maintaining" the level of mediocrity they have achieved that they will not risk one iota of what they have.

It's like the young boy who, at long last, got his first pair of really fine shoes. Now, these shoes were exceptionally fine. So fine, in fact, that the boy spent many hours wiping and shining them while keeping them safe from scuffs, neatly wrapped in paper, in their box under his bed. A number of opportunities presented themselves for the boy to wear the shoes, but he chose to safe-guard them and wore his older shoes instead. After all, if he wore them, he would run the risk of scuffing them or dulling their glittering shine. When the day finally arrived when the occasion was most important, the boy learned, to his disappointment, that his feet had grown and the shoes no longer fit him.[*]

Unfortunately, most people are like that boy. They read all of the books, booklets, plans, and programs about the principles and techniques used by others to gain success. As the boy did with the shoes, they let the opportunities to use what they have learned pass them by or they make a half-hearted start, but never continue past their first small and futile attempts.

Why do they hold back?

Because they fear losing what little they have. They "protect" their meager and mediocre position so well that they never lose it.

At retirement age, those people look back with pride at the

---

[*] I gave that pair of shoes to a more needy neighbor and, from that day forward, have never again been afraid to lose anything.

fact that they have ventured little and lost nothing. But, not unlike the boy and his shoes, they learn, to their disappointment, that that which they protected so well will not sustain them after their retirement and they are forced to seek aid and assistance from their government, family, and friends.

In order to succeed, you must first *lose your mediocrity*. Success doesn't happen any other way.

Have you ever wondered why people (like you) pursue money-making business opportunities?

It usually begins with a need or desire for more money, but…

If it was only about making more money, you could get an extra or better job. That, however, would subject you to the same lack of freedom inherent in any job.

Opportunity seekers aren't just seeking more money. They are seeking the freedom to come and go as they please; pursuing the pleasures and luxuries of life only available when you have money enough to afford them.

"If your only goal is to become rich, you will never achieve it," said John D. Rockefeller, a man who knew a little something about making money and getting rich.

Unfortunately, the sad truth is that the vast majority of people spend their entire life seeking because they want their freedom, but are unwilling to give up their imagined security.

So, how do you combat the opposing thoughts since your mind can only entertain one of those thoughts at a time.

You could chant some mystical incantation you have learned in some other mind-stuff writing, but that would only give you another thought to occupy your already overloaded mind. You would have three, instead of just two, thoughts competing for your single (and only) attention.

Being a human being, regardless of what you do, you will consider any possible losses in any undertaking in which you will be involved, as we all do. It is the same with any goal you may choose, especially money making endeavors.

How then do people (like me) with the same concerns of possible losses overcome what the motivational writers call the "Fear of Failure" or the "Fear of Loss"? Are we, somehow, more risk-averse than you are?

It has been often repeated that entrepreneurs (like me) are the risk takers in the business world. Entrepreneurs are supposed to make great gobs of money by taking risks and enjoying the profits, but that ain't necessarily so. Entrepreneurs only take *calculated risks*, not just any risk.

Even today, with my over fifty years of practical, hands-on business experience, any time I contemplate a new venture, I consider any and all possible losses that may arise from that venture, just as you would. I ponder each possible loss (failure) and determine whether or not I can accept that loss.

I also do something else—something far more important—before I accept it as a calculated risk.

As I consider each possible loss that my arise from that venture, I ask myself one very important question.

What would I do if that loss (failure) happens?

By having a specific plan of action—a *contingency* plan—in place for a possible loss, the thought of such a loss can be eliminated or, at least, ameliorated. It then becomes a calculated risk—a risk that I can not only endure, but survive.

In other words, I am prepared for that possible loss.

If, however, I cannot come up with a viable contingency plan that will allow me to be prepared for a possible loss, I don't take on that venture.

Then again, being prepared may become another venture unto itself, a venture that will allow me whatever is needed to create a contingency plan. That could be time-consuming, but I would have to measure the cost in time against the possible profits from the venture originally being considered.

Unfortunately, over the years I have found that most people never do any contingency planning for *anything*. They simply consider the possible losses and abandon their goal.

They don't know—or understand—the words of Lloyd Jones: "The men who try to do something and fail are infinitely better than those who try to do nothing and succeed."

Think about that.

12

Write It Down So You Don't Forget

Write it down so you don't forget. It's something you need to do. Unfortunately, all too many people figure they don't need to write it down, because "I can remember that. After all, it is my goal, isn't it?" Maybe so, but as a member of Mensa—the society for people with an IQ in the 99th percentile—I know that that and $1 will usually get me a cup of coffee.

So, I write notes to myself everyday. Some of the notes are goals to accomplish, things to do, things I need, and some are just quotes, comments, or ideas.

If you ever visit my office, you will find those little, yellow sticky-notes on my desk, on my calendar, on my computer, or on my wall. Once I accomplish the goals I have set for myself, did the things I needed to do, got the things I needed to get, after I have re-read the quotes and comments enough times that they are embedded in my sub-conscious, and I have moved the ideas to my ideas book, I discard those notes.

So, no matter how smart you think you are, *write it down so you don't forget.*

All of the mind-stuff writers and motivational gurus tell you that you should write down your goals and re-read them every day, morning and evening. That's a very good idea, but I do it a bit differently.

I write it down five or six times each day!

Some years ago, I found that just re-reading what I had written could too easily be interrupted by other thoughts and, because my mind can only think one thought at a time, my mind would succumb to those thoughts.

By physically writing down my goals each and every time I think about them, my mind is preoccupied with only those thoughts relating to those goals.*

For instance, way back when (that's a *long* time ago), remembering what I had learned from Ed in Cabbage Hollow, I wrote down my major goal so I wouldn't forget it. Then, I remembered that Ed also told me to "forget about looking for answers. Learn to ask the right questions. Just remember the words of Rudyard Kipling...

"I keep six honest serving-men

"(They taught me all I knew);

"Their names are What and Why and When

"And How and Where and Who.

"Not an answer in the bunch. Just questions. If you ask yourself the right questions, the answers will come to you."

So, after writing down my major goal—"I will get rich"—I began **ASK**ing myself the questions to which I needed answers. As those answers came to me, I wrote them down, too. Most of the answers to those questions changed as I matured in the pursuit of my goals.

Two of the most important questions I asked myself were

Why do I want to get rich?

and

What will I do when I get rich?

The answers to those two questions changed often until I finally settled upon a worthwhile reason to get rich and what I proposed doing once I became rich.

---

* I always write everything down in cursive. I mention that because I don't know how effective printing will be since they are no longer going to be teaching cursive writing in the schools.

No matter what your goal may be, you must at least answer those two questions: Why do you want to achieve that goal? *and* What will you do when you have accomplished that goal?

The reason you need to find answers for those two questions is in order to give your goal a *purpose*—a reason for which you want what you want. Without a purpose, your goals will only be hollow wishes and dreams. As I learned as a lad back in Cabbage Hollow, your goal is "where you are going." Why you are going there and what you will do when you get there completes the plan for your trip.

Once you have established your purpose for your goal, which will change and have to be rewritten as you mature in the pursuit of your goal, begin asking yourself the other questions as defined by Rudyard Kipling which, of course, will change and have to be rewritten during your trip to your ultimate goal.

As you ask those questions, also determine and write down what physical actions you will need to do in order to find the answers.

I think I just heard someone say, "Didn't you forget something important? *Don't you have to include an absolute certain date or time by which you will reach your goal?*"

Back when I was much, much younger, I followed that advice from the mind-stuff gurus, too, but do you know how demoralizing it can be to reach that date and not see your goal achieved?

As an example, I once wrote down that I would be a millionaire by my 25th birthday (I put in the actual date). On my 25th birthday I was not quite a millionaire, but I was well on my way so I rationalized that I was achieving my goal and I was just a little late. On a weekend shortly after my 25th birthday, my business was burglarized. The burglars had stolen all of my inventory and everything else of any value. I had to start all over again.

From that day onward, *I only set dates certain for the accomplishment of physical actions*. In other words, I would set a date certain by which I would do a certain physical task necessary to the achievement of my ultimate goal. Each time I completed the required physical task, I was one step closer to achieving my goal.

How do you eat an elephant? One bite at a time.

If you have the faith of a mustard seed, you can move mountains…If you get a shovel and start hauling the mountain away one shovel full at a time.

In order to write down my goals, purposes, and the answers to the multitude of questions and any changes to my answers, I kept a spiral notebook entitled "Goals." In that notebook there would be entries that were crossed out and new entries made. That notebook grew in size over the years.

No, I did not write down everything in my goals notebook five or six times each day. I simply wrote down my goal—"I will get rich"— which focused my mind on all of the writings in my notebook.

I would, of course, re-read the entries in my goals notebook frequently and update the answers to my questions as needed. I'm sure some of my teachers thought I was a little nuts when they found that goal written on so much of my school work. They were sure I was nuts when I also wrote "I will have a new Cadillac"! By keeping my goals notebook and updating it, I kept my mind and actions focused on the achievement of my goals.

Start your own goals notebook today. Keep it updated as you seek the answers you need to achieve your goals.

Write it down so you don't forget.

13

The Third Mind

What about those times when the answer to almost every question asked seems to just jump into your conscious mind. You even seem to know the answers to questions you didn't even know you knew.

We used to call it being "in the groove." My grandsons say they are "in the zone." No matter what you call it, it is a delightful experience. It's like you can do no wrong. You just seem to know what you need to know without even thinking about it.

How do we sometimes remember things we didn't even know we knew?

Since we know the sub-conscious mind is a phenomenal recording and play-back mechanism, if at anytime in our life we have encountered that question, the answer will be played back to us.

Then again, what if, in reality, we have never had any exposure to that question or answer. Where would the answer come from?

That, then, begs questions about Extra Sensory Perception, metaphysics, psychic phenomenon, telepathy, mind reading, psychokinesis (mind over matter), or the law of attraction causing the desired outcome of events in your life and business—accomplishing impossible goals.

All of the mind-stuff writers will state emphatically that the sub-conscious mind produces those results. We know, however, that the sub-conscious mind does not—and can not—initiate any activity. It can only play back what it has recorded.

The mind-stuff writers, as usual, are somewhat right because the sub-conscious mind does play a role in such phenomena; but, as always, they overlook the physical side of the equation: that grey mass enclosed between your ears. Your brain. I call it the *Super-Conscious*.

Electroencephalograms, which trace and record the structure of the electrical activity of the brain, prove the brain itself is an electrical mechanism. As such, it is capable of transmitting thoughts and intentions to create a desired response or reaction. The brain also functions as a receiver, accepting input to our conscious mind.

Beyond that, studies of psychokinesis—the ability to move things or otherwise affect the property of things with the power of the mind—have demonstrated an influence over dice and random number generators.

We won't even go into the studies in quantum physics.

We exert this brain power over everything in our environment. Because we are unaware of it, instead of acknowledging it, we deny it. That is where the sub-conscious mind comes into play.

Once your conscious mind has accepted the fact that something can be done or can happen, that possibility can be recorded in your sub-conscious. Of course, you can not record the possibility that something can be done if you can't believe it can be done. In other words, don't try to convince your conscious mind to believe that pigs can fly. They can't and you know it.

Having consciously accepted the possibility that something can be done, you must then consciously accept that *you* can do it or it can happen for you. That is when the super-conscious begins searching for a source or resource to bring that possibility into existence.

All you have to do is consciously direct your super-conscious to find the answer.

Even though your super-conscious may find the sources or resources you need, it cannot bring those sources or resources into existence for you until **you do something to make it happen.**

You can't pour water from an empty bucket.

If your goal is to own a new home, your super-conscious cannot search for that new home unless it has a place to search. In other words, you will have to investigate homes for sale in the area in which you want to live. Then, your super-conscious will be able to search to find what you want.

If your goal is to be rich, you can't do it sitting in front of the TV waiting for money to fall from the ceiling. You must do something to make the money you want or need. That's why, when I decided I wanted to be rich, I spent countless hours in the public library studying everything and anything about doing business and making money.

As Albert Einstein said, "Anyone can be a genius if they pick just one specific subject and study it diligently just fifteen minutes each day."

I think I just heard someone say, "Oh, yeah? What about winning the lottery."

That goes back to the "faith of a mustard seed." If you cannot truly believe and have faith that you will win the lottery, it can't happen for you. Of course, you must buy a lottery ticket, too. The same belief and faith must be present in any task you set for your super-conscious.

Most of the mind-stuff writers offer physical positions you must assume or breathing exercises you must follow in order to achieve the results you desire. None of them are necessary.

Since your super-conscious is active all the time—twenty-four hours a day, seven days a week, even while you sleep—it isn't necessary to turn it on—and you can't turn it off.

Once you believe and have faith that what you want can be yours and have prepared yourself by doing something to make it happen and consciously directed your super-conscious to find the sources or resources required, just go about your daily affairs while your superconscious does its work.

When the conscious command is made, the sub-conscious mind plays back the sequence of actions that must be taken and the super-conscious begins seeking the resources needed to accomplish your purpose.

The only prerequisite is this…

You must be brutally honest with yourself!

You may lie to others and get away with it but you know when you are lying to yourself and that lie will be recognized by your sub-conscious mind. That same lie will sorely limit the ability of your super-conscious to do your bidding and accomplish your goals.

Thought is the original source of all wealth, all success, all material gain, all great discoveries and inventions, and of all achievement.

—Claude M. Bristol

14

The Master Mind

Have you ever heard of the "Master Mind" concept? Napoleon Hill, in his book *The Law of Success*, explains it this way.*

"A Master Mind may be created through the bringing together or blending in a spirit of perfect harmony of two or more minds. Out of this harmonious blending the minds create a third mind which may be appropriated and used by one or all of the individual minds. This Master Mind will remain available as long as the friendly, harmonious alliance between the individual minds exists. It will disintegrate and all evidence of its former existence will disappear the moment the friendly alliance is broken."

Anytime you have a conversation with, or correspond with, a person with whom you share common interests, goals, and ambitions, in a spirit of perfect harmony, you *will* create a third mind between you—a "Master Mind," a mind upon which you may both call for insights neither of you may have even known existed.

That is the most powerful wealth building secret ever told!

Without the Master Mind, there is no success, even for those people who do not know about, or accept, the Master Mind concept.

As a matter of fact, the reason I wrote this chapter to begin with is because of a dear friend of mine. He is a successful, wealthy

---

* Although Napoleon Hill is credited with the Master Mind concept, it actually predates his writings by about 2,000 years. "For where two or three are gathered together in my name, there am I in the midst of them." (Matthew 18:20)

man. In a conversation with him a couple months before this was written, when I mentioned the Master Mind concept, his response almost floored me. He said, "I don't believe in that hocus-pocus."

When I explained to him the "real" Master Mind, he readily admitted that it was the personal contacts he had cultured over the years that had allowed him to make his fortunes in a number of businesses (as have mine). In his words: "I always thought that Master Mind stuff had something to do with metaphysical, psychological motivation."

It seems almost everyone, even those who espouse the use of the Master Mind, are locked into the metaphysical, psychological motivation concept, ignoring the physical application that actually guarantees your success in business and life (as explained in this book).

Just imagine you are faced with a major dilemma in your business. The situation seems to be "do or die," but you don't know whether you should "do" or "die" or find an alternative.

Wouldn't it be wonderful to be able to pick up the telephone and call someone who has either faced the same dilemma or knows someone who has. The "real life" experiences shared with you would be worth far more than anything you could read in a book.

In the words of U.S. Supreme Court Justice Thurgood Marshall: "None of us has gotten where we are solely by pulling ourselves up from our own bootstraps. We got here because somebody bent down and helped us."

Then again, what if you were thinking about getting involved in a new venture you had just read about. The opportunity sounded exceptional, but the promoter offering the opportunity only talked of the benefits and rewards. Knowing that *all* opportunities have inherent risks associated with the possible rewards, you pick up the telephone again and begin asking the people you know "Have you ever been involved in a venture like this?" or "Do you know anyone who has ever been involved in a venture like this?" What you learn may save you from losing your shirt or you may learn that the rewards in that venture far outweigh the risks and you will be able to go into that venture with prior knowledge of those risks (risks you didn't know about before you **asked**).

Or, what if one of the people you know telephones you to ask "Do you know anyone who might be interested in buying a boxcar full of new, excess widgets?" You may have to answer "I don't know," but an honest answer from you, even if it is "I don't know," is far more valuable than gold.

On the other hand, you might know someone who might know someone who may be interested. In that case, you have the option of either freely giving that name and telephone number to the person you know or telling them, "I might know someone. Let me check it out and get back to you." If your search comes up with a real, potential buyer, you can negotiate a fee with the person you know and earn a finder's fee for the introduction. Then again, if your search doesn't come up with a possible buyer, you will pay the person you know the courtesy of calling back to say you couldn't find anyone.

That kind of personal, one-on-one interaction is how real fortunes have been made for all recorded business history and are still being made today by those of us who align ourselves with other business people and opportunity seekers like ourselves.

Like Daniel Webster said, "Man is a special being, and, if left to himself in an isolated condition, would be one of the weakest creatures; but associated with his kind, he works wonders."

Wouldn't it be wonderful if you had a notebook of your very own filled with the names, addresses, telephone numbers, e-mail addresses, and pertinent details about people with whom you share common interests, goals, and ambitions? People who not only shared your interests, goals, and ambitions, but were willing to share their life experiences with you?

What are you waiting for?

Start building your own Master Mind notebook today. Fill it with kindred spirits: people like yourself who are doing something to accomplish their goals with full knowledge of the risks and potential rewards inherent in the opportunities you pursue.

Where do you find those people?

They are everywhere. In every business (small or large) in the world; in every store, shop, or business establishment you frequent; and on every business discussion board on the Internet.

Back when I was young and super-active in business building

my empire, I kept a small spiral notebook with alphabetical dividers. In that notebook I kept the names, addresses, telephone numbers, and pertinent information about people I knew in business, the professions, and service industries.

Although I knew a lot of business people from all industries and walks of life, the only ones I added to my notebook were those who were actively doing something to better their way of life and were willing to share their experiences with me.

I'd be willing to bet that Henry Ford, J.C. Penney, J.P. Morgan, John D. Rockefeller, Joseph Kennedy, Howard Hughes, Ted Turner, Donald Trump, and even Bill Gates have had notebooks similar to mine.**

Each person had a full page in my notebook with information about how I had come to know them; when and what I had done for, or with, them (if anything); what they had to offer; what they might need; anything and everything I learned about them updated every time I learned something new.

I even had pages filled with other *accommodating**** "opportunity seekers" like me who were doing something to accomplish their goals and were willing to share their life experiences with me. Why? Because everyone knows somebody and, statistically, in this country, you are only three people away from anyone else in the country. That means that someone you know knows someone who knows someone who knows whoever you want to know.

That notebook was the foundation upon which I built fortune after fortune in business after business over the past fifty-plus years.

Any time, over the years, when I was faced with a business method or concept I didn't fully understand or needed to find someone to accomplish a specific task, I would turn to my notebook and ask those people who might know.

"How does this work?"

"How do I do this?"

** I know for a fact that Sam Walton of Wal-Mart had one because I was in it and he was in mine.

*** I did not include wannabes who were only looking for a free lunch and never at the very least offered anything in return.

"Where can I find this?"

"Have you ever had dealings with this guy?"

"Could you check this out for me?"

"Do you know anyone who can do this?"

At the same time, I was always available to respond to the same kind of inquiries from them.

Remember what W. Clement Stone said. "If there is something to gain and nothing to lose by asking by all means ask!"

A young man who owns a small, local dry cleaning business has been added to my personal "Master Mind Notebook." The very first time I met him, he shared some information about an advertising idea he had with me and asked me for my opinion. That's how I met him. Over the years, I have used the very same technique in order to find those people with whom I could build a rapport. I have shared some of my own ideas with other business people and asked for their opinions. If those people responded by offering to share their life experiences with me, we were soon in each other's notebooks.

Better than forty years ago, I shared one of my ideas with a man I happened to sit next to on an airplane. We were both headed for Chicago and struck up a casual conversation. When he asked what I was going to do in Chicago, I shared with him the opportunity I was pursuing at the time. Since he appeared to be a businessman, I asked him what he thought of my idea. Although he admitted that the idea was outside his personal knowledge, he encouraged me to try it anyway, because, in his words, "The worst that can happen is they'll say no."**** Before we got off the plane in Chicago, we exchanged business cards and went our separate ways.

A couple weeks later, the man I had met on the plane telephoned me to ask what had happened with my idea. After I explained to him that my idea had been rejected, he told me he had asked one of his friends about my idea and his friend thought it might work in a little different way. He shared that man's name and telephone number with me. The idea didn't work even then, but over the next ten years, until his death, he and I called each other frequently to share ideas with each other. Little did I know, until

---

**** Which they ultimately did.

years after his death, that he was, at the time I met him on that plane ride, one of the wealthiest men in Chicago.

Beyond that serendipitous encounter, in a number of instances, I have read a book, booklet, report, or article that paralleled my own thoughts, opinions, or experiences. After reading those writings, I wrote to the authors thanking them for sharing their insights and offering some of my own thoughts on the same subject. In most cases, the authors didn't respond; but in cases where they did respond, by and large, they in turn shared their further experiences with me. Some (not all) of them ended up in my Master Mind Notebook—and I in their's.

You never know where or when you will meet other "business people" or "opportunity seekers" with whom you may share common interests, goals, and ambitions—kindred spirits, your counterparts, fellow travelers on the same road. Get to know them. Let them get to know you. Share your life experiences with them. Let them share their life experiences with you. **Be forewarned:** if you are unwilling to share with them openly, honestly, and freely, you can expect nothing in return from them. In the words of Napoleon Hill: "This Master Mind will remain available as long as the friendly, harmonious alliance between the individual minds exists. It will disintegrate and all evidence of its former existence will disappear the moment the friendly alliance is broken."

There you have it. **The most powerful wealth building secret ever told!**

Please use it wisely and pass it on to those who, like yourself, are seekers of opportunity—with all the inherent risks and potential rewards.

"What you keep to yourself, you lose; what you give away, you keep forever." So said Axel Munthe.

Now, here's *the Inside Secret of the Master Mind*…

My Daddy once told me, "There are no secrets in this old world. Just things you don't happen to know, yet." So, what I am about to tell you is only a "secret" because you don't happen to know about it—until now.*****

***** I will continue to use the word "secret" for what I am about to tell you for lack of a better word.

Allow me to again quote what Napoleon Hill in *The Law of Success* wrote...

"A Master Mind may be created through the bringing together or blending in a spirit of perfect harmony of two or more minds. Out of this harmonious blending the minds create a third mind which may be appropriated and used by one or all of the individual minds. This Master Mind will remain available as long as the friendly, harmonious alliance between the individual minds exists. It will disintegrate and all evidence of its former existence will disappear the moment the friendly alliance is broken."

Let me also add: "For where two or three are gathered together in my name, there am I in the midst of them." (Matthew 18:20)

Within those two writings is an even *greater* secret.

Although that secret should be obvious to anyone reading it, the secret seems to be overlooked by those who both teach and practice the Master Mind methodology. Observe...

There is no such thing as a Master Mind *group* and there never can be.

What?

I know. I know. Almost everyone who teaches or practices the Master Mind method espouses the joining together in "groups" in order to generate, and benefit from, a Master Mind

But it *cannot* happen.

Why?

Although Napoleon Hill wrote that "two or more" minds can create a Master Mind, the much earlier writing limits the affect to "two or three" only.

There is a reason for the limitation on the number of people who can generate and benefit from a Master Mind—the reason, in fact, why there can never be a Master Mind "group."

Have you ever been involved in any group activities? In school? Church? Chamber of Commerce? Lodge? Fraternity? Sorority? Sports? Whatever?

I'm pretty sure you have.

When you participated in those groups, have *all* of the people in that group shared "perfect harmony" with each and every other member of that group?

If you answered yes, you need to be more observant.

Any time you are in a group of more than three people, there is always at least one person who is *not* in "perfect harmony" with the group or *not* in "perfect harmony" with some other member of the "group." When that is happening, the Master Mind can never manifest itself.

As Napoleon Hill wrote, "*This Master Mind will remain available as long as the friendly, harmonious alliance between the individual minds exists.*"

Go ahead! Try to get more than three people to be in "perfect harmony" anywhere at any given time about anything. It just doesn't happen.

When even one mind in a group isn't in "perfect harmony" with the others, a Master Mind can not be generated. That's why there is no such thing as a Master Mind group and there never can be.

By your personal, one-on-one interaction between yourself and only one other person (or at the most, two other people) at a time will you be able to generate, and benefit, from the Master Mind created between you. Each alliance between yourself and one or two other people will open the doorways to your future successes and generate multiple Master Minds for your mutual benefit.

You now know a secret that seems to have been overlooked by most of the Master Mind scholars.

Success in business and life is dependent upon *what you know, who you know, who knows you,* and, perhaps most importantly, *your willingness to share with your fellow travelers.*

Keep in mind what Ralph Waldo Emerson wrote: "It is one of the most beautiful compensations of this life that no man can sincerely try to help another without helping himself."

15

How to Get Rich

How do I get rich? That's the question that I am asked the most.

Here's how I did it.

Step by step.

1

I learned very early in life that the *only* way to make money was to "sell" something. Either a product or a service. Something people wanted or needed. Or do something for them they couldn't, or wouldn't, do for themselves.

I think I just heard someone say, "I don't have to sell anything. I have a job!"

Whether you want to know it or not, you are "selling" your time, talent, and ability to your employer. Beyond that, your "job application" was the advertising you used to sell yourself.

2

I learned to "make do" with what I had until I could get what I needed to do a better job.

Wouldn't it be wonderful if you had all the fixtures, gadgets, tools, and equipment you needed to begin with?

Unfortunately, most people don't have the money available when they first start to get everything they think they need. So, in too many cases, they decide to wait until they have what they think they need before they start.

I remember vividly building the display shelving for my first retail store because I couldn't afford store-bought shelving. Even after I could afford "professional" shelving, I kept the shelving I made because it worked just fine and I figured why should I meddle with a good thing?

I learned that I had to do anything necessary (but legal) to get to where I wanted to be, even if I didn't like doing it—*especially* if I didn't like doing it. You must do *anything* you need to do until you can do what you want to do.

"Start by doing what is necessary, then do what is possible, and suddenly you are doing the impossible." Saint Francis of Assisi said that.

I learned to never ask anyone to do anything for me that I wasn't willing to do myself and everyone who has ever worked with me has taught me about what they have done for me and how they did it. After a while, I could do it, too, but maybe not as well as they did.

When my Daddy told me not to ask anyone to do anything for me I wasn't willing to do myself, I said, "Oh, yeah. I can't have a baby myself."

His answer completed the admonition, "I didn't say you had to be able to *do* it yourself. I said you had to be *willing to do it* yourself. If you ask a woman to have your baby, you should be willing to have a baby for her—if you could."

I learned to pay for what I wanted. If I couldn't afford it, I saved-up to be able to afford it. Sometimes it seemed like forever. As a matter of fact, the higher the cost and the longer it took me to save-up for it, the more valuable it was to me.

I learned that no matter how long it took to achieve my goal

(whatever it was), it would have been just as long if I hadn't persisted, but I would have accomplished nothing. Remember Benjamin Disraeli who said, "The secret to success is the constancy of purpose."

7

I learned that *nothing* is as easy or as fast as it should be. It only gets easier and faster when you know how to really do it—and learning how to really do it is just a matter of doing it over and over, and over until you finally find out how it works. Of course, if you give up after the first (second, third, or fourth) try, you'll never do it.

"That which we persist in doing becomes easier to do. Not that the nature of the thing has changed, but the power to do it has changed." That Ralph Waldo Emerson was a pretty smart guy, wasn't he?

Here's another smart fellow: Aristotle. "We are what we repeatedly do. Excellence, then, is not an act, but a habit."

8

I learned most of what I know from my mistakes and failures. My successes never taught me anything. They were only based upon what I had learned from my mistakes and failures. That's why those who are afraid to make mistakes or fail never achieve the success they desire.

"Success is a lousy teacher. It seduces smart people into thinking they can't lose." Bill Gates said that and he's someone who should know.

9

I learned that my most prized possessions were my customers, people who, directly or indirectly, paid for my lunch every day. That's why, unlike my contemporaries, I reply to my customers e-mails personally. The customer may not always be right, but a customer is always a customer.

10

I learned that money is *not* an end unto itself. It is only a way of keeping score. The saddest people in the world are those who are forever chasing the almighty dollar and the vast majority of them have no real respect for money.

To quote John D. Rockefeller: "If your *only* goal is to become rich, you will never achieve it."

11

I learned to ask for what I wanted or needed and to graciously accept a "no" as readily as a "yes." Remember the lesson I learned from Ed in Cabbage Hollow: Forget looking for answers. Learn to ask the right questions!

Yes! You can get rich, but you'll have to do it yourself. No one will do it for you!

I get tickled by people who want to start at the top of the ladder. For some unknown reason, they honestly believe they are better than I am, since I had to start on the bottom rung and climb up one rung at a time.

When I mention the above, I often hear "Yeah, I could do that, but it will take too much time. I need money now and I don't want to just make a little money, I want to get rich."

Sorry, friend. You'll have to start where I started.

Do what you need to do to make a little money.

Then, do more and more of it to make more and more money.

As you make more and more money, the greater the opportunities you will have to make even more money.

Nothing succeeds like success—even small success.

The more things you don't want to do, the fewer and fewer things you will do, until you are doing as most people do: Nothing but dreaming!

I can teach you how to do it, but you won't get it until you actually start doing it yourself.

Remember what the great inventor Thomas Edison said. "Our greatest weakness lies in giving up. The most certain way to succeed is always to try just one more time."

Mustard Seeds, Shovels, & Mountains

Most people spend all their life looking for money in one form or another. They look for it in the strangest places and under the weirdest conditions, but they never seem to find it. The sad part is they really have more money than they ever imagined; they just don't know it.

If you don't know what money is, how can you expect to get someone else's money to use?

So, before we can get down to the nitty-gritty, there is one lesson you must learn. It's not a hard-to-learn lesson, but most people never learn it and go through life looking for something they already have.

Money is only a medium of exchange.

That simply means that *anything* that can be exchanged for something else is **money**.

Until you finally learn and accept the fact that *anything* (and I do mean anything) you can exchange for *something else* is money, you will be doomed to a life-long futile search for something you already have. Let me tell you a true story about George*. He "borrowed" a whole factory.

---

* George is a real person, but, since his company is still in business and I'm sure he wouldn't want a bunch of crazy telephone calls interrupting his business days, I have not given you his last name or where his company is located. I've also used generic terms to describe his business rather than the specific product lines, just in case you're in the same kind of business and might recognize him from clues in his story.

When I first met George, he was a successful manufacturer of an industrial product. That's a product that is sold to other manufacturers who use it to manufacture other products. One day, in my office over a cup of coffee, we were swapping war stories about our various business activities. After telling George how I had started my business, he told me how he had "borrowed" a whole factory to start his business.

Before he was a manufacturer, George was a salesman, selling the same industrial product he later started manufacturing. He was a pretty good salesman and made enough to support his wife and seven children comfortably, but not lavishly.

George had always dreamed of owning his own factory. He had approached a number of lenders, but had always been turned down. The money he thought he needed was just too much for his provable "limits."

By the way, one of the reasons George was a successful salesman was because he was (and is) a meticulous record keeper. He made it his personal responsibility to take exceptional care of his customers. And, his customers knew they could depend on him because he had proven it over and over again in their dealings.

When George celebrated his 40th birthday, he started considering where he had been, where he was, and where he wanted to be. If he was going to make his dream come true and own a factory of his own, he had better get moving or he would be too old to enjoy it later.

Taking a look over all of the packages and proposals he had prepared for various lenders over the years, George made a list of all the things he thought he needed to get his factory going. After he had that list, he went through it again and again. Each time, he eliminated more and more of the nice-to-have items, until he had a bare-bones list of only the most necessary items. That list included:

1. Incorporation of the business
2. A building to work from
3. Office equipment and supplies
4. Manufacturing machinery
5. Employees
6. Raw materials and supplies
7. Operating cash

Everything on his list could be had with "cash," but George didn't have and couldn't get that kind of cash. So, he "borrowed" all of it, one piece at a time, until he had all of it.

To get started, George felt he had to, first, incorporate a business. Since George didn't have cash for the attorney's fees and filing fees, he talked to a friend of his who was an attorney. After George explained that he was going to manufacture the same product he had been selling for about twenty years, the attorney prepared the corporate charter, paid the filing fees himself, and agreed to act as Secretary of the corporation for ten thousand shares of the company stock (out of 1,000,000 authorized shares). After all, he knew George could sell the product and make a profit, if he could manufacture it.

George's proven skill of selling the product had gotten him one item on his list. Only six more to go.

Down the road from George's home, there was an old, run-down mill building. It had a railroad siding, loading docks, and even a set of old truck scales, but it was really in a sorry state of disrepair.

George had driven past that old building thousands of times. He really hadn't noticed it until he started looking for a building for his factory. The only real reason he noticed it even then was because, after pricing buildings for rent or purchase, he had all but given up on finding a building he could afford.

The owner of the building lived in a house on the other end of the property. The old building had been there when he bought the property about ten years before. He had meant to do something with the building, or tear it down, but he just never got around to it.

After a number of conversations, the owner agreed to let George use the building for a period of two years, rent-free. During that time, George would repair the building, make it usable and presentable, and clean up all the debris that had accumulated around the building. At the end of two years, George would either vacate the building, leaving all of the improvements, or he would enter into a rental agreement with the owner at $1,500 per month for the next three years.

George had his building, but it was far from being serviceable. Working nights and weekends, with help from his wife and children, George managed to get the building cleaned-up inside and out. At work during the day, he enlisted the help of other salesmen. At church on Sundays, he enlisted the help of his friends.

As time went by, more and more of his friends helped-out with the painting, wiring, plumbing, and general fix-up of the building. A friend of a friend who worked for the telephone company even put in an extension of George's home telephone since it was less than a half mile from George's home. The old building took on a new life, much to the amazement of the property owner.

While George and his friends were working on the building, his brother-in-law closed a small branch office of his insurance brokerage. Since his brother-in-law didn't have a place to store the excess office furnishings, George told him about the factory. George borrowed the office furnishings, including an almost-new typewriter.

George was well on his way. He had his business structure, building, and office. An empty factory doesn't produce much product, though.

Because George had worked in the industry for a good many years, he knew most of the manufacturers. So he knew that two of the manufacturers had replaced some older, out-dated equipment with brand-new equipment over the past two years. Maybe one of them would have some used equipment he could get.

Talking to the two manufacturers, George discovered that between the two, they had enough old equipment to set-up one full production line. Although neither of them would agree to let George just "use" the equipment, they both agreed to allow him a one-year option to purchase. George would move the equipment to his location and at anytime during the year, he could pay for the equipment or arrange financing. If George did not buy the equipment within one-year, he would be required to reimburse the companies for the use of the equipment at a set rate per month on each piece of machinery and pay all costs involved in returning the machinery (if he didn't have someone else to buy it).

Actually, the manufacturers were so glad to get the machinery out of their buildings, they used their own labor and trucks to deliver the machinery to George at his building.

It's one thing to have machinery, but yet another to operate it. Especially when you don't have any cash money to cover payrolls for employees!

Talking to some of the machine operators at the other factories, George made a deal with three of them to run his machines for him in the evenings and on weekends. Since he didn't have any cash money to pay them salaries, he made an agreement with them to pay them a percentage of each order produced and shipped. This way, they would get their pay as soon as George was paid for the products they produced.

After he had his machinery installed and ready to operate and had his signed agreements with his part-time employees, George went after the raw materials and supplies he would need to manufacture his product.

By showing the suppliers of the raw materials and supplies through his factory, George was able to get them to agree to ship their materials and supplies on a 90-day billing cycle. That meant he would have 90-days to pay for those materials after the materials were delivered. But, George could only get the materials he would need to fill each order. Therefore, he would have to show the suppliers confirmable purchase orders before they would ship the goods.

George quit his job and went on the road selling the same products he had been selling for years. This time, though, he was selling for his own company.

As George got purchase orders from the buyers, he took them to the raw materials suppliers so they could be confirmed. The raw materials and supplies were shipped on the agreed-upon 90-day billings.

When the raw materials and supplies were delivered, George notified his part-time employees. They produced the product and shipped it to the buyers.

Even though George invoiced his customers on a net 30-days basis, there was a time lag between billing the customer and receiving payment. During that time lag, some things that George couldn't borrow had to be paid for with cash money. Such things as electricity and gas were increasing in direct relation to the amount of manufacturing being done. And, the freight lines that delivered the product to George's customers required cash payment or George's product wouldn't be delivered.

To get the cash money he needed to cover operating costs, George ran a classified ad in his local newspaper, something like this: "PRIVATE INVESTORS WANTED for going manufacturing concern with orders in hand and production scheduled. Call George at 555-1111."

Although the response to the ad wasn't very big, George showed each of those who responded his new factory, the purchase orders he had in hand, and delivery slips and invoices on the product already manufactured and shipped. George sold enough of them some of his stock at $1 per share to cover his cash operating cost until the cash started coming in from the billings already made.

George had "borrowed" a whole factory.

When you finally accept the fact that money is *anything* you can exchange for *something else*, you may be able to do even greater things than George did. All you have to do is break your desires down into their basic component parts. Then acquire each of those component parts using someone else's money in whatever form it may take.

Of course, you should *only* use someone else's money for things you really need. Beyond that, you must always remember that when you do use someone else's money, you take on a responsibility far beyond any you would bear using your own money. If you misuse someone else's money, you will pay penalties that could be disastrous to your financial position for many years to come. And, it doesn't matter whether the money you use is "cash" or something else of a tradable value.

Believe it or not, I have just revealed to you some of the most powerful tricks, techniques, and methods used in the world of business and finance. Tricks I have used over and over myself to build my own fortune. The beauty of those methods is that anyone can begin using them immediately to achieve financial independence.

But, I'm not going to itemize and annotate them for you.

If I were to itemize and annotate the various and many tricks, techniques, and methods, you would simply nod your head and never use the information. But, if you really want that knowledge, you'll read and re-read this chapter until the knowledge you seek strikes you like a bolt of summer lightning.

Anyone can get all of the money they need—someone else's money—when they finally learn what money really is.

First, you must consciously accept the fact that it can be done.

Then, you must believe that you can do it.

But, the results will only come when you do something to make it happen.

That's **Physio-Psychic Power**.

And that's how you really and truly move mountains.

Epilogue

In all religions, the faithful are constantly admonished to "read your Bible every day"—or whatever Holy Book the religion adheres to.

Unfortunately, too many people read a book once and, thinking they know everything it says, never open it again.

Those who really succeed read and study their "bibles" every day—re-reading those books that relate to whatever they are doing.

I, myself, have some books I read and re-read on an on-going basis. Beyond that, whenever I am involved in a business or situation I have been involved in before, I go to my archives and re-read my notes to remember what I have done; or should have done.

So, no matter in what endeavor you are involved, read your "bible" everyday!

Try it.

You will find that you learn (or re-learn) something every day.

On the following page is a list of books that I think could become good "bibles" for you—in addition to the book that you are currently holding, of course. While this is by no means a complete list, it should serve as a good starting point for you.

Recommended Reading

The Magic of Believing	Claude M. Bristol
TNT: The Power Within You	Claude M. Bristol
The Richest Man in Babylon	George S. Clason
The Secret of the Ages	Robert Collier
Science and Health	Mary Baker Eddy
How to Be Rich	J. Paul Getty
The Master Key System	Charles F. Haanel
Think & Grow Rich	Napoleon Hill
Life Is Tremendous	Charlie "Tremendous" Jones
How to Succeed in Business by Breaking All the Rules	Dan Kennedy
Psycho Cybernetics	Maxwell Maltz
The Master Key Workbook	Anthony R. Michalski
I Believe Therefore I Am	Claire McGee
Atlas Shrugged	Ayn Rand
The Success System That Never Fails	W. Clement Stone

You can find all of these book in bookstores, online, in traditional book format, in e-book format, priced high, priced low, and even free. In other words, you won't have to look far to find them.

In addition to these books, I am also an advocate of reading biographies and history books.

Finally, don't be afraid to partake in some "light reading." We all need to take some time to recharge our batteries. I would also be lying if I didn't admit to getting a business idea (or two) after reading a good spy novel.

The important thing for you to do is to read, reread, and then reread as necessary until you thoroughly understand how this "stuff" works. Or, until you get rich. Whichever comes first.

You Can Be a Millionaire in One Year or Less

You can be a millionaire in one year or less right in your own home town from your home (or office) in less than five hours per week while you keep your current job or business (if you want to) without any kind of e-mail list or website. Do it just as I have for over fifty years—and I made my millions before we even had computers, long before the Internet existed. So, let me ask you…

Do you want to be a millionaire?

There are more opportunities to make **big money** easily and quickly in your hometown than there are on the Internet—and making that money takes less time and far less aggravation, too. (Have you mastered HTML, javascript, RSS feeds, PHP, website creation, autoresponders yet? I'm still working on it myself. You really don't have to learn all that computer stuff to be a millionaire in one year or less. All you need is e-mail, the most basic of computer skills, and PDF files! All of which would make you more money than you could imagine.)

Over the past fifty years, I have generated over $500,000,000 in revenues by simply knowing the buyers and giving them what they want or need. I was a millionaire before most of today's Internet gurus were even born!

My old computer still has a mailing list with over 700,000 known buyer's names and addresses on it. The only problem with those buyers is they only buy "one at a time."

Right now, there are a number of promoters talking about "niche marketing." That's where you find a "niche"—people who regularly buy a specific product or service. Then you find or develop a product or service that the people in that "niche" might want or need. When you have something they might want or need, you sell it to them.

But you still have to find the buyers. And...

Just like most of my 700,000 buyers, you can only sell them one product or one service at a time. It's good money, but it is also a great deal of work.

I still do it every day, but my **big money** has always come from a few hundred known buyers and a few good deals each year. I don't have to "sell" them anything. I just tell them I have what they want and they buy it.

Right now, there are probably 50 to 100 known buyers just like them in your home town. And, I know where you can find another 200 or more without any real effort. You don't have to "sell" them anything. Just tell them you have what they want and they will buy it from you—and they usually won't be buying just one of anything.

I had been doing this on my own for over fifteen years when a friend of mine—doing much the same thing—suggested we pool our resources to increase our profits. We did and our individual incomes skyrocketed. Some of the fees we earned would boggle your mind. We never told any outsiders what we were really doing.*

Later, other men and women who were doing much the same thing joined with us. Our individual fortunes grew exponentially.

With all of the "known buyers" my friend and I had, the other members of our group were forever amazed, but we never told anyone what we were doing or how we were doing it.

We took an oath never to tell anyone.

My friend is now retired and I ain't getting any younger, so, with my friend's permission, *I am now revealing our long-held secret to the next generation of aggressive entrepreneurs.*

Being an incurable entrepreneur, I used my money to buy a bank, a gold mine, a printing company, a coal mine, a steel fabrication business, and a number of other businesses—all the while writing, printing, and selling my own information about doing business and making money.

---

* Before I started writing this, I asked my ol' friend if I could use his name. He politely declined. So, throughout this report, he will only be identified as "my friend." He did agree to allow me to tell you what he and I had done and how we had done it—something we had never revealed before (except to our kids and grand kids).

Back then, in our group, each of us had "known buyers" for a wide variety of products and services. So, when one of us would come across a hot deal, we would simply share it with the others then split the profits (sometimes to the tune of hundreds of thousands of dollars) when one of our "known buyers" bought.

As you can imagine, one of our biggest expenses back then was the cost of communicating with each other by telephone, Telex, and overnight delivery. My communication costs regularly ran from $1,000 to $2,000 *per month*. It was costly and it limited our group to only those who could afford it.

When fax machines became available in the 1970s, our expenses dropped but the cost of a fax machine back then still limited our group to those who could afford the machines—and not all of us had fax machines. My first fax machine cost $2,700. Today, you can buy a fax machine that does even more than my first one did for less than $100.

Recently, another old friend of mine, a member or our group, telephoned me out of the blue to see what I was up to these days. We reminisced for about an hour about the good ol' days, deals we had done, people we had known, money we had made, and airplanes we had owned. Then, he made a comment that got my juices flowing. He said, "If we had e-mail communication and everything they have now back then, we could have made ten times the money in half the time."

When I suggested that we put the old group back together using Internet communication, he laughed. I had forgotten that most of our group were either retired or dead. (Sometimes I forget how old I am.)

For about a week after my conversation with my old friend, every time I thought about what he had said, my juices started flowing. The more I thought about it the more I wanted to get my old group started up again. So I contacted what few of them I could find.

You guessed it. They loved the idea, but were too happy being retired to get involved. Some of them suggested that their grand kids would be better prospects, but their grand kids really didn't have the necessary entrepreneurial spirit. Then, one of them suggested, "Why don't you teach some young entrepreneurs to do what we used to do and put together a group for them."

An absolutely brilliant idea! So, that's what I have done. But…

When I began investigating the possibilities, I found a variety of "opportunities" that offered to "buy and sell" closeouts and liquidations for you. They even offered to finance the deals and share the profits with you.

After reading three of those plans, I was totally disappointed. They all told you "what" to do, but they never really got around to telling you *how to do it*. Beyond that, closeouts and liquidations are only the very small tip of the iceberg. Besides, postings on some of the discussion boards indicated that the promoters never financed any deals and never sold anything to split the profits.

In other words, they told you what to look for and provided some form of "submission sheet" so you could send what you found to them. One of them even demanded that you send a "sample" or your submission wouldn't even be considered (after paying nearly $3,000 for the service).

As Colonel Potter on *M*A*S*H* used to say: "Horse Pucky!"

Why do you need anyone to finance your deals? Members of my old group rarely, if ever, put any of our own money into any deals. Some of us (like me) did, simply because we could make more money financing our own deals, but we only did it when we had gobs of money to play with.

Why do you need someone to "sell" the deals for you? If you have "known buyers," you never really have to sell anything. Just tell them you have what they want.

Why should you limit yourself to closeouts and liquidations? Closeouts and liquidations are only the tiny tip of the iceberg. Why not used equipment (of any kind), boats, yachts, ships, airplanes, antiques, classic cars, scrap metals, guns and ammunition, furs, diamonds and other precious gems, automotive and aircraft parts....

And the list goes on and on...from A to Z...from everyday items to the most exotic.

Anyone can find the "sellers" of those items, but only those with "known buyers" can make a profit. **When you know the buyers, *then* you can be a millionaire in one year or less!**

My old group is now dead or dying and I'm getting older every day. Soon, there won't be any of us left to pass on our methods to a new generation of aggressive entrepreneurs. So, as my last hoorah,

I have decided to teach you the methods and techniques my generation of entrepreneurs used to make tons of money right in our own home towns, from our homes (or offices), in less than five hours per week, while keeping our jobs or businesses, without any kind of e-mail list or website (didn't even have them back then).**

You Can Be a Millionaire in One Year Or Less!

In *You Can Be a Millionaire in One Year Or Less!* I take you by the hand and teach you exactly what we did with point-by-point, step-by-step instructions—with letters, forms, and e-mail messages you can use—showing you exactly *how* to do it—and I teach how to do it using today's Internet.

You Can Be a Millionaire in One Year Or Less! will teach you...

+ How to identify the "known buyers" in your home town (they're everywhere).
+ How to "know" what they need or want.
+ How to contact them (no guess work!) with actual letters, e-mail messages, and forms you can use.
+ Why those "buyers" need you more than you need them.
+ How to get the products and services they want or need (again, no guess work).
+ How to form your own group to expand your resources nationwide—even world wide or you can just use the "new" group I have set-up for you.

And that's just the tip of our iceberg.

In *You Can Be a Millionaire in One Year Or Less!* I reveal some closely guarded secrets that, until now, I have only shared with my kids and grand kids.

You will learn why my friend and I almost always had a buyer before the others in our group even began looking—and we *never* told anyone what we were doing or how we were doing it. Until now.

You will even learn the simple method we old guys used to generate from $500 to $1,000 per week. I'll even give you a source we

---

** As my old friend suggested, with e-mail communication and every other technology available nowadays, you can make ten times the money in half the time. With those communication advantages we never had, your fortune is practically assured.

didn't even have back then. We used to call it our "bread & butter money"—money we could use to pay bills, finance a deal, or whatever, until the next deal came along. (That method alone could earn you two or three times your current salary working only five hours a week instead of forty.)

As soon as Rebecca Hagel read her copy of *You Can Be a Millionaire in One Year Or Less!*, she sent this out to her readers:

> Jim Straw handed me a package of reading that's actually caused me to wake up in the middle of the night thinking about it. Since he's getting older, Jim decided to do a final "hoorah" and finally lay out **exactly** how he's made millions of dollars over the last fifty years.
>
> He claims if you use the material you too can be a millionaire in less than a year. I confess: I don't like income claims like that because I'm afraid a regulatory body will come and wrap his knuckles. However, without making any income claims, let me just say this: I'm so impressed that I got to work immediately using his strategy.
>
> Does it work?
>
> Eight years ago I dabbled in one little bitty part of this and yes, it worked, sometimes to the tune of hundreds of dollars in a week. Now, Jim's report just completely opened my eyes to the possibilities. I was playing in a kiddie pool back then.
>
> I hope you'll join me in this venture, because as it turns out working in a group actually increases your income.
>
> —Rebecca Hagel

Barry Rice wrote this to me:

> Jim, your **You Can Be a Millionaire in One Year Or Less!** now has my wife mad at you and me both. We'd been planning on bumming around for a couple of months in our RV, but now that (in the three weeks since I purchased your program) I've

earned $17,351 on my first two deals, I've delayed our trip a bit. Trying to tell her that if we just wait and I'll buy her a larger one from what I will earn with your program just isn't cutting it. Her response, "We have one of the largest RVs made now. What're you going to do, buy one in a different color?"

Jim, I've been around the business block a time or two myself, however, your "Millionaire" program provides an all new blueprint to putting some easy cash in ye ole bank account. And, I haven't even completed your recommended minimum of three readings yet. Combining your "Millionaire" program and your "Snooping Around" program is the cat's meow when it comes to making some of the easiest money I've made—and I've also made a bunch through the years.

One of the exciting aspects I've found with your "Millionaire" program is that it opens the 'brain cells' to an all together new form of creativity in seeking the easiest and fastest ways to go from initial idea to putting cash in the bank. Adding a bit of a twist to one of your suggestions, I've uncovered what is looking like will be a steady source of "buyers" and "sellers." As a matter of fact, this source(s), plus a couple other ideas I've had already has had a few potential "buyers" calling me. And, that's just by working in my local area.

As you know, I teach seminars, training programs, and offer my own downloadable program that guides folks to achieving their own definition of what success will be in their future. But, even if I didn't, I can confidently say that with your **You Can Be a Millionaire in One Year Or Less!** program, if the person will stop merely wishing, start doing something, ASK questions, is committed to earning a million dollars, follow your plan, and add a cup and a half of creativity…the million bucks WILL be there.

If my wife has her way, it might be that I won't

earn my Million Dollars in one year with your program—but, it'll only be because she throws all my
business stuff, business cards, and laptop out the RV
window as we are heading down the road.
—*Barry Rice*, http://www.bwrenterprises.com

Barry made $17,351 in just 3 weeks! When you order *You Can
Be a Millionaire in One Year Or Less!* Barry shares that twist and
those sources with you.

J.M. Sirvent in Spain wrote to me…

> *Less than one week of work, only two clients,
> and one single product will mean 180,000 Euro +
> 250,000 Euro. I have been dedicated 15 years to cor-
> porate finance and have closed deals for 250 million
> Euro, but I am very seriously changing my business
> as this is simplicity. In addition, I did a 25,000 Euro
> in real estate, again with only two days of dedication.*

By the way, the "Euro" is the European currency at about US$1
per Euro, maybe a little less today, but still a sizable piece of change
for only three deals.

It really does work in almost any business—and, if you ask (after
you order the course), I'll even help you adapt it to your specific business.

This fellow tripled his sales in 60 days!

> *Jim, I read over your Be-A-Millionaire course
> more than the three times you recommend. I knew
> it would work but my current business is my main
> concern, so I adapted your method of finding buyers
> for my current business.*
>
> *All I did was adapt your letter and send it out to
> all of my current customers along with the form. The
> response was fantastic.*
>
> *Now I know what my customers want to buy,
> how many they want to buy, and how much they are
> willing to pay. Most of it was stuff I am already sell-
> ing. My sales have tripled in the past 60 days.*
>
> *You may tell your readers about what I've done*

but PLEASE don't use my name or location. I don't want my competition to find out what I'm doing.
—Anony Mouse

Maxine Allen (Slough, 15 miles outside London) tells me...
With the help of my solicitor and your course, I contacted a seller and put them in contact with my client, the buyer, with the agreement that I would get 5% finders fee . This process took a total of three months, from Feb 2008 to the end of May 2008. This may not sound like a lot to you or any of your students, but I'm ecstatic! I made £5,097 with just one deal over three months (because I was lazy). Imagine if I had knuckled down and took on three deals at a time? I just work in my living room/office after I've finished work (of which I'm planning to hand in my notice in a few weeks).

By the way, £5,000 is about $10,000 in U.S. dollars.

Don't just try to "survive" during the current financial crises! Turn it into an opportunity to make your personal fortune. Get my personal help making tons of money during the current financial crises, recession, and coming depression. Let someone else teach you how to just "survive" if that's all you want.

During times of financial crises—like now—opportunities to make big money increase exponentially. As a matter of pure fact, there were more fortunes made during the Great Depression of the 1930s than at any other time in our history or since.[***]

You Can Be a Millionaire in One Year Or Less! is real, not some pie-in-the-sky horse puckey. I've been doing it for fifty years and I don't just tell you what to do, **I tell you how to do it**— point-by-point, step-by-step, with the actual words you need to use to

---

[***] When you order your personal copy of *You Can Be a Millionaire in One Year Or Less!* you will also receive "The Inside Secret to Making a Fortune During Financial Crises, Recessions, & Depressions." This special report will never be sold as a separate report at any price. It is only made available to those who have taken my *You Can Be a Millionaire in One Year Or Less!* course. You have never read anything like this before.

make it work for you.

You Can Be a Millionaire in One Year Or Less!—complete with all the bells and whistles—is only $997, a small price to pay for fifty years of experience. That's fifty years you won't have to spend learning what I know.

This is my last hoorah. I ain't getting any younger. Order your personal copy today. *You Can Be a Millionaire in One Year Or Less!*

Keep well,

J.F. (Jim) Straw

P.S.

Someone recently asked, "If it's so profitable, why not just do it yourself instead of writing about it?"

Well, I have been "doing it" for over fifty years and still do.

Let me ask you this: why do mathematicians write math books? Why do medical doctors publish their methods? Why do plumbers, electricians, composers, architects, and even hobbyists write handbooks and instruction manuals?

We write down our methods for the younger generations, so they won't have to learn for themselves how it's done as we did: by trial and error.

Included!: Membership in the Mercantile Connections Exchange

When you order your personal copy of *You Can Be a Millionaire in One Year Or Less!* you will also get a lifetime membership in the "Mercantile Connections Exchange," my new "group." Regular Membership Dues are $240 per year, but your membership is included and will be yours for life.

Personal Mentoring from Me

When you order *You Can Be a Millionaire in One Year Or Less!* you will have me as your mentor—personal advisor—for as long as I am alive. I will personally read and personally respond to your e-mails. I won't have some flunky do it. And I won't just field your questions about the course. *I will be personally available to you to assist you in any business endeavor.*

No matter what business you're in, whether you're just starting, well on your way, or at the top of the heap, I've probably been where you are and done what you are doing. So, what is your biggest problem in your business right now? Let me help you solve it.

Extra Bonuses Included!

Finder's Fees: The Easiest Money You'll Ever Make
> My all-time best seller—over 50,000 copies sold—updated in 2006 to include how finders can use the Internet. Sells for $100 everyday.

Sell American
> Start your own export business for a couple hundred dollars. Your very first order could easily return your investment ten-fold (or more). Sell American is a "how I did it" and "how you can do it, too" book based on real life experiences in international trade. Sells for $99.^{95} everyday.

Exactly How You Can Make a Fortune Just Snooping Around
> Every once in a while just plain dumb luck can make you a fortune. That's what happened in this case. I made over $1,000,000 in less than 60 days just snooping around. Sells for $29.95 everyday.

How To Get Filthy Rich Selling Real Estate You Don't Own!
> How can you sell something if you don't own (buy) it first? What could be better than controlling a real estate empire without buying any real estate? Sells for $29.^{95} everyday.

Please Note!

When you receive *You Can Be a Millionaire in One Year or Less!*, read it at least *three times* before beginning your business.

Although the specific letters and forms included in this course will work to produce the results you need, you will also learn how the buyers and sellers think. Beyond that, you will learn why my friends and I did the things we did—the kind of entrepreneurial thinking you will not find in any other money-making course, not even any of the college level business textbooks.

Read it! Study it! When you finish, you will know why and how...

You Can Be a Millionaire in One Year or Less!

Order safely and securely now at

www. businesslyceum.com/BeAMillionaire.html

or use the order form supplied here...

☑ **Yes! I want to be a millionaire in one year or less!** Please e-mail the course to me at the e-mail address supplied here. Enclosed is a check for $997 or you may use the credit card information provided to charge that amount. I understand that my purchase is completely guaranteed by you and I will let you know if I have any problems or questions. I will read *You Can Be a Millionaire in One Year Or Less!* no less than three times when I receive it and I will take advantage of my Mercantile Connections Exchange membership and your personal mentoring.

Name		
Address		
Address		
City	State	Zip
Country (If applicable)		
Phone Number		
E-mail		

If paying by credit card, please complete the following:

Credit Card #	Expiration Date	Security Code

When completed, please mail this form to:
J.F. (Jim) Straw
204 Wildflower Way
Dalton, GA 30720-8029

If you have any questions, please e-mail *jfstraw@businesslyceum.com*.

Who Is J.F. (Jim) Straw?

J.F. (Jim) Straw began his long, successful career in business at the age of nine when he sold his first cans of Clover-leaf Salve and copies of *GRIT* newspaper. Even at that early age, he had the unique talent of recognizing an opportunity, implementing a plan, and making a profit.

Jim's career progressed through direct selling, service contracting, wholesale merchandising, entertainment (he was a professional trumpet player, vocalist, and radio announcer), freight forwarding, import/export, retail merchandising, warehousing, real estate, electronics manufacturing, finder's fees, closeout merchandising, financial brokerage, business consulting, steel fabrication, gold and coal mining, offshore banking, mail order, writing, and publishing.

Over the past 37 years, J.F. Straw has written well over 700 books, booklets, manuals, reports, courses, and articles about doing business—all based on his own personal, hands-on experience. His writings are specific methods, techniques, and approaches to doing business that anyone can use to start or expand their business.

J.F. Straw has sold over five-hundred million dollars ($500,000,000) worth of products and services by mail—everything from beauty supplies to heavy equipment, burglar alarms to sleeping bags, fishing lures to women's wigs, automobiles to wheelchairs, investment opportunities to seafood, consulting services to "how to" courses.

You can learn more about Jim at *www.JFJimStraw.com*.